Children Dancing

A Practical Approach to Dance in the Primary School

Rosamund Shreeves

Ward Lock Educational

ISBN 0 7062 3832 X

First published 1979
Reprinted 1982, 1983, 1985

Set in 10 on 12 point Baskerville
by E. Williamson & Son (Printers) Ltd.
and printed in Hong Kong
for Ward Lock Educational
47 Marylebone Lane, London W1M 6AX
A Ling Kee Company
Hong Kong · Taipei · Singapore · London · New York

Contents

Part I
General

Movement Content

The Lesson

Starting Activities

Exploring and Developing Movement

The Dance

Accompaniment

Part 2

Stimuli (general)

Flash Cards

Movement Patterns

Objects

Dressing Up

People

Moods and Emotions

Animals

Nature

Seasonal Events

Shapes and Sculpture

Sound

Poetry

Stories

Myths from Other Countries

Pictures

Colourful Locations

Machines

Work Dances

Games

Part 3

Imagery and Action Words

Movement Patterns

Objects

Dressing Up

People

Moods

Animals

Nature

Seasonal Events

Shapes and Sculpture

Sound

Poetry

Pictures

Colourful Locations

Machines

Games

Appendices

Photographs

These photographs were taken by Terry Williams at Strand-on-the-Green Junior School, Chiswick. They show inexperienced children practising some basic dance actions.

Foreword

This book comes at a time when thousands of young people are turning to the performing arts in the hope of discovering what the daily round does not seem to be able to offer them. Never has there been more dancing of every imaginable kind since we were known world wide as 'the dancing English' and never have more books been written about the subject. Over forty years ago the educational system recognized the need for the personal and creative life of the child to be given more scope, but these aims become increasingly difficult to achieve when competitive selection at an early age becomes the hurdle to 'getting on', and the 'equal opportunity' becomes the race for place. Miss Shreeves offers here a veritable encyclopaedia of dance material and class organization set out in such a way as to act as a ready reference and a mine of ideas for teachers who have little or no time to re-create themselves on the job and perhaps little energy for a replenishing hobby in their free time. But it is much more than this. This book is for all those who love children and dancing. Underlying all Miss Shreeves writes is her own delight in dancing with and for children and in playing such colourful games with them that each child can go off on his own magic journey, coming back for more only when they need to. I have seen her in action, and I know that Miss Shreeves's book was born out of her need to share with others her own joy and satisfaction in creating something together. Never has a book of this kind been more timely. The earlier children can enter into the real world of experience, the more hope there is for the future.

Jane Winearls

Part I

Part 1

General

1 INTRODUCTION

Making dance is as valid as making music or making stories. Although dance enriches many other activities, it does not need to be justified in any terms other than itself.

Many people nowadays are rediscovering the need to dance and the happiness this brings them. Dance is a unifying activity involving the whole self. It is both disciplined and spontaneous. To dance is in the deepest sense of the word to *be* more vividly. Self-awareness grows with movement awareness.

Curt Sachs writes about the need to dance as 'an effervescent zest for life'. This children certainly have. In dance, many children experience release and satisfaction not found in any other activity.

Dance can spring from anything in human experience. The basis of dance is broad and far-reaching, but the *expression* is always in terms of movement. Rhythmic movement is the raw material of dance: the rhythms arise out of the movement and the impulse to dance. A dancer uses rhythms and shapes in the same way that a painter might use colours and textures.

Dance is concerned with evolving rhythms and patterns of movement which can symbolize or represent human activity. In this way it is different from mime or drama.

2 DESCRIPTION OF THE BOOK

The book is intended as a practical guide to the teaching of modern dance in the primary school. Part 1 describes movement content, i.e. what to dance about and methods of working. Part 2 shows how movement content can be related to a wide variety of stimuli. Part 3 is a collection of lessons exemplifying Parts 1 and 2. They are intended as detailed examples of both movement materials and methods of working. Some suggestions for 'follow-up' work in different media are included in this section. (See Index for detailed cross-references.)

The movements and examples are deliberately simple. Action words drawn from everyday language are used to communicate and stimulate movement. It is hoped that the visual effect of the action words will help the teacher to 'feel' the rhythm and quality of the movement herself.

The book is not intended as a comprehensive study of movement, but as an indication of a way of working. Basic movement concepts are developed and repeated throughout the book, giving plenty of opportunity for assimilation and repetition. Directed movement examples go alongside creative work in order to encourage both bodily skills and movement imagination.

It will be evident that there is much cross-sectioning of stimuli. Any one stimulus could invariably be linked to another, so that the teacher may need to read several sections to clarify her idea. The numbering throughout should facilitate this. Where relevant, music, poetry, reference books and follow-up activities are mentioned in the text and also listed in the Index.

The book need not be read straight through. Some may find it easier to read a few lesson examples and then refer back to the general headings in Parts 1 and 2.

3   AIMS

The main movement aims in this book are:

   (a) a flow of action
   (b) a variety of action
   (c) increasing movement skills
   (d) individual creativity and achievement.

To relate movement meaningfully to anything in the child's environment or experience, and to encourage similar ways of working in other media.

4   THE TEACHER

The teacher provides specific movement ideas. She is both instigator and guide, and she plans the lesson so that the children have an opportunity to become deeply involved in a variety of movement. It is essential to *plan* in advance both the movement and the sort of accompaniment that is to be used.

In each lesson the teacher directs many of the movement phrases, both to ensure that a movement is fully experienced and also to give models on which variations may be built. The balance between freedom and imposition is only achieved after much practice. Dance is essentially a 'doing' activity with creative interaction between teacher and children.

5   INVOLVEMENT AND INTERACTION

The teacher must be fully involved with the movement and the children. It is through sensitive interaction, suggesting, observing, guiding and responding that dance teaching takes place. This is not always easy, but movement generates energy. To become involved is to become refreshed. The teacher does not have to dance fully, (she can use her hands, and voice) but she must in the early stages be feeling with, not standing back and observing. There is a place for that later on when the children are more experienced and secure.

The ability to dance well oneself does not necessarily denote a good dance teacher. A less skilful but sensitive teacher can guide children towards expressive, clear and formulated movement. This book provides a simple basis of ideas; using this as a starting point, the teacher's knowledge and awareness can grow alongside that of the children.

6 EXCITEMENT

Children who are fully involved in movement will be excited in the sense of being enlivened. To dance is to move more precisely and more fully than in everyday life. Movements are repeated for the enjoyment of the rhythmic sensation. Vitality and energy are aroused. The child's sense of his whole physical being is heightened.

Unless the teacher gives clear movement directives, and fully involves the children, their energy becomes purposeless and they lose concentration. This is what sometimes happens and teachers then lack confidence to repeat the lesson. It is important to state clearly when the children are to begin *moving* and when they are to *stop*. (The muscular experience of stillness is as important as that of moving.) She can also state clearly whether they are to move *on the spot* (in place) or *travel* about the room. Conversely if the teacher does not fully involve the children, lethargic action and inattention can result.

7 MOVEMENT AS THE KEYNOTE

Sometimes teachers will rely on story and mimetic movement as they feel these may hold the children's attention better; however, it is the excitement of the story and not of the movement that does so. In dance, it is the movement ideas themselves which must generate excitement and enthusiasm.

8 VOICE TO ACCOMPANY

The use of the voice is very important. The teacher can suggest *what* the children are to do and, by using the voice expressively, can communicate *how* they are to do it. The teacher's voice is in one sense 'doing' the action the children are experiencing. Just to say 'walk' or 'stretch' will not communicate the essential nature of the action and the children may move with little involvement. The voice can be the rhythmic accompaniment to the action and it is the rhythmic content of movement that involves and vitalizes. For example, draw out the word:

s - t - r - e - t - c - h!

making sure that the children are really extending as far as they can. Or use a firm rhythmic and accented quality in the words:

Walk, walk, walk and *turn!*

Say the words or make voice sounds. Use the voice in any way to make the movement flow in phrases.

9 PERCUSSION TO ACCOMPANY

Playing a percussion instrument is another useful way of communicating. Teachers can easily learn to play simple movement rhythms.

Play the instrument to indicate when to move and when to be still. The children can move to the sound of the instrument and stop when the instrument stops or vice versa (the latter is very dramatic). The instrument can indicate the rhythm and nature of the action, showing whether, for example, it is a large, strong action or a quick, light one: tap quickly and lightly and stop for:

Run, run, run, run, run, run and balance!

The use of percussion is indicated in many of the lesson examples (see also **46-51**).

Find different ways of playing percussion instruments which will correspond to different types of actions. For example, a drum can be banged, tapped, smoothed, played loudly or softly.

Movement Content

10 AN ANALYSIS

No matter what the stimulus for the dance may be it is the oppor-
tunities for movement and the logical development of that movement
which should determine the course of the lesson.

Movement can be defined simply in the following ways:

What you do— actions of running, jumping, skipping, tumbling,
stretching etc. using different body parts and body shapes.

How you move— quickly, smoothly, strongly, slowly, lightly etc.

Where in the space around you?—up, down, forwards, sideways,
etc. to the right or left.

With?—in relationship to: a partner, a group or an object.

These are the four aspects of movement. Any movement can be
defined in these terms by asking:

> What is the action or the part of the body involved?
> What is the quality of the action?
> Where does it go in the space?

Using this analysis, action can be improved or varied (see **33-37**). For
example:

> To improve: 'Lift your knees high as you skip. Lift your heads.'
> To vary: 'Try skipping sometimes forwards, sometimes backwards'.

This poem (from *'Peepshow' A Little Book of Rhymes* by Pamela
Blake) exemplifies the idea:

> The High Skip
> The Sly Skip
> The Skip like a Feather
> The Long Skip
> The Strong Skip
> And the Skip All Together

11 ACTION WORDS

These define what the body or parts of the body are doing. The
following is a list of words for movement and stillness. Throughout
the book, there are many indications as to how the teacher can deepen

5

the awareness of the action. The list includes all the basic ways of moving but is not meant to be definitive.

walk	stop	slither
run	settle	slide
skip	freeze	rush
gallop	hold	dodge
leap	pause	zig-zag
hop	hide	dash
jump	listen	dart
roll	look	drift
crawl	balance	float
bounce	hover	skim
stand		stride
lie	dive	glide
kneel	melt	fly
	flop	tip toe
open	fall	stamp
close	pounce	clap
grip	crumple	jab
strectch	duck	push
swing	plunge	pull
turn		smooth
twist	explode	cut
	toss	shake
	shoot	hit
	reach	throw
	rise	whip
	shrink	tap
	grow	
	spread	

The action words act as catalysts in the creative situation: they start off movement invention.

They can also be used to give *practice* in movements; for example, bouncing can instigate a *creative* task: 'How many ways can you bounce?' Or they can be used to increase skill: 'Can you stretch your ankles, lift your body as you bounce?'

Dances can be made using action words as a basis.

12 UNDERSTANDING ACTION WORDS

Children may not be familiar with the action word. The true understanding of the movement and the word comes from 'doing'-over and over again. The teacher may communicate the ideas through her hands, an object, a rhythm, or any of the many ways indicated in the book. Words can arise from movement and be used to define it. There is constant interplay between language and movement; the one enriches the other. Children become interested in words that describe their movement.

Young children spontaneously use words to accompany themselves and will suggest colourful words like 'swirling' or invent new ones like 'clumping'.

13 ACTION PHRASES

Action phrases or sequences evolve naturally from a sense of what movements 'go together'. The growth of one movement to the next must be *felt* in the muscles. Help the flow of movement with the accompaniment. Give children sequences to practise and help them to discover their own phrases in creative movement. Dance is about the *relationship* of one movement to the next, one rhythm to the next and one person to another.

Gradually encourage the children to build longer sequences and more 'aware' action where the body parts, shapes or rhythm are clear. The more skilful the child, the more he will be able to *link* actions together and also to *combine* actions, for example:

> linking—run and jump and fall
> combining—skipping with opening and closing the arms.

From an early age children delight in rhythmic phrases of dance. A four-year-old said:

> I can swing and move and dance
> I can swing and stretch and arch.

14 VARIETY

'To dance is to move . . . more fully than in everyday life.' Therefore children must be helped to feel the extremes of their movement, to feel the contrast of reaching out into the space and curling up small, to feel the release of leaping high and the contrast of moving low. Every lesson should contain contrasts and variety. Only the teacher can judge the length of time that should be allowed to develop a particular activity. Very young children tire quickly and need to work in short phrases of activity and rest.

Consider the action-word list in terms of contrast.

15 GOING AND STOPPING CONTRASTS

In dance there is constant interplay between moving and stopping; different ways of moving, different ways of stopping; energy being expended and gathered again. Rhythm and phrasing in dance arise out of this muscular feeling of when to move and when to be still.

Link moving words with stopping words to make simple phrases of movement and accompany them on a percussion instrument, or with your voice, for example:

running and balancing   Practise running lightly and easily, balancing and lifting the body, feeling the moment to run again.

stride and freeze   Practise striding firmly, stopping firmly.

skip and listen   A phrase of skipping, pause, and wait to hear the accompaniment before skipping again.

bounce and hide   Practise bouncing high and hiding (crouching) near the ground.

Stopping words

    freeze

    pause

    settle

These words encourage an awareness of different types of stopping. 'Look' helps the children to think ahead to where they are going to move next in space.

Make rhythms of going and stopping phrases. Repeat them over and over at one time so that the movement really 'gets going'.

16 BODY-PART CONTRASTS

Movement contrasts can be demonstrated by using one part of the body after another, for example:

    the hands can clap

    the feet jump

    the arms swing

or by performing contrasting movements with one particular part, for example:

    the feet stamp, jump and slide.

Make lists of body-part action words. The children can make an enormous drawing of the body and label it with action words. Note how many of the actions can be performed by the whole body or part of the body.

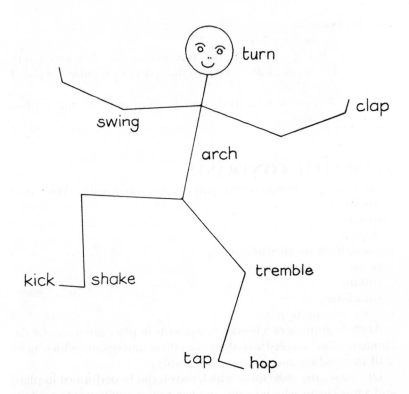

Phrases of body-part action words can be practised in the classroom and in the movement lesson. Placing emphasis on different body parts makes the children *feel* them more vividly. Many of the 'lessons' stress movement of body parts.

17 QUALITATIVE CONTRASTS

Action words may stress the qualitative (the 'how?') aspect of movement and give a movement experience of speed or slowness, strength or lightness, for example:

glide
explode
rush
pounce

The ability to move with these qualities of movement will develop after much practice and repetition in many different dance situations.

The above actions might be practised by the whole body or a body part, for example:

glide—ith the fingertips

(sitting) 'Bring your fingertips together so that they touch very gently. Let them glide away into the space, then come back and touch again gently.'

Many qualitative words arise from looking and touching, from poems and stories.

18 SPATIAL CONTRASTS

Contrast *travelling* movement with *in place* movements. Words like:

leaping

rolling

skipping

are *travelling* words whereas:

rising

sinking

stretching

suggest moving *in place*.

At the beginning of a lesson, movements in place often *involve* the children more successfully than travelling movements which need skill in avoiding and giving way to others.

Of course, any movement which travels can be performed in place and a movement which begins in place may develop into travelling, for example:

bouncing on the spot *or* travelling

rising and sinking *as* you travel.

Other spatial contrasts involve change of *direction:*

forwards

backwards

above

around

and changes of *level:*

high or low movements which contrast moving into the air or along the ground.

Encourage children to move fully in the space all around the body.

19 RELATIONSHIP CONTRASTS

Try to vary too in the lesson whether the children are dancing by themselves, with the teacher, or a partner. Help them to dance with others as well as alone.

20   A DIAGRAM OF MOVEMENT CONTRASTS

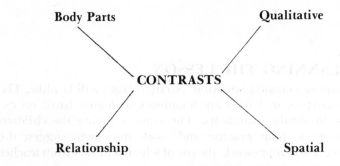

Body Parts   Qualitative

CONTRASTS

Relationship   Spatial

Of course no one lesson contains all the contrasts! (See the suggested lessons in Part 3 for examples.) Contrasts ensure an ebb and flow of energy, a balance between activity and rest, excitement and calm. This balance in the lesson is far more important to the success of the lesson than any stimulus. A particular type of contrast might be stressed over a number of lessons.

The Lesson

21 PLANNING THE LESSON

The lesson is a creative situation. No two classes will be alike. The lesson examples in Part 3 are imaginary dialogues based on experience in similar situations. The aims of giving the children opportunity to both *practise* and *create* movement suggest the following lesson framework, the use of which will vary from teacher to teacher and situation to situation.

Each part of the lesson may be freely interwoven with another. Some lessons may be mostly directed with a little creative work towards the end. Some lessons may stress exploration in movement while others concentrate on making a dance; selecting and consolidating ideas. Whatever the stress, try to end with some corporate movement which will draw everyone together. With young children the culmination of the lesson might be a simple unison movement with the teacher. Older children enjoy making dances of their own which can be improved and added to over several weeks.

In planning the lesson consider:

1 *Starting activities* to encourage concentration and body awareness and to improve movement skill (see **24-32** for details).

2 *Exploring and developing movement*—individual creativity (see **33-37**).

3 *Making a dance*—selecting an idea or ideas from the central part of the lesson and clarifying a beginning and ending (see **38-45**).

4 *Accompaniment* (see **46-51**).

22 A LESSON EXAMPLE

The children kneel near the teacher, arching and curving their backs. They stand and practise rolling and stretching in place. They travel about the room with stretching leaps and a clear change of direction. They flop for several minutes. They explore falling and rising as a movement idea. This leads to a variety of sequences.

They build partner dances from the above ideas, to which they give titles like 'nightmare', 'slow motion' or 'ambush'.

23 DIAGRAM OF THE LESSON PLAN

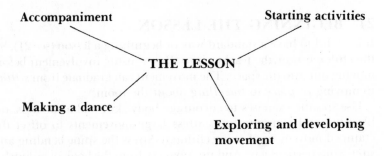

Accompaniment   Starting activities

THE LESSON

Making a dance

Exploring and developing
movement

Starting Activities

24 BEGINNING THE LESSON

It is useful to have a standard way of beginning a lesson (see 21). Sit the children near the teacher initially to ensure involvement before moving out into the space. The movement can graduate from *sitting* to moving *in place* to *travelling* about the room.

Use specific exercises to encourage body skill and awareness, or listening and concentrating. Stress large movements to offset the cramped movement of many children. Stress the spine bending and stretching particularly. And use imagery from the book or colourful language to communicate the idea. Use repetition and clear accompaniment.

25 RELAXATION

Contrast different types of movements, otherwise children become tense. Practise relaxing, flopping out on the floor or letting the head hang down, keeping the legs straight. Encourage movements that flow easily from one to another. Rhythmic ability is blocked by tension. Encourage 'allowing the rhythm to happen'.

The following lists can be used as a basis for ideas. Select two or three ideas to suit the age and experience of the children. Use Contrasts (15-18) for further ideas.

26 SITTING OR KNEELING MOVEMENTS

Make sequences.

Hand movements	open them wide
	grip them tight
	rotate the wrists
	finger tips on the floor
	(and lift them high)
	wrists on the floor
	palms on the floor
	shake them all about
	press the palms together and relax
	(repeat)
	(feel this movement in the whole body)
Head	drop and lift from side to side
	(floppy head) circle and lift

Shoulders	lift and *drop*
	circle
	quick shrugging
Arms	stretch high over head (reach for the sky)
	drop down
Back	sit straight with a long back
	drop the head down to the feet
	arch the back and look up
	turn and look behind as far as possible
	look forward again (this twists the spine)
	sit holding the feet. 'Walk' the feet
	forwards
	The arms are straight and head goes to
	the knees.
Copying	the teacher's body part
	copy hand, elbow, hand movements
Slow motion	body-part movement. The children
	choose:
	elbow moves
	head moves
	hold the shape you are in. Remember it.
	Stand and find a space on the floor sit in
	the remembered shape.
Clapping	a rhythm:
	clap it with palms, finger tips, wrists,
	clap it high, low, to the side.
	clap it on the knees, floor, head
Moving and stopping	to an Indian bell sound
	fingertips part and come together again
	softly
	slow head movements
	slow arm movements
Two contrasting sounds	on a tambourine
	bounce hands or feet
	shake hands or feet
Counting	moving over different length phrases
	stand slowly over six beats
	sit down over six beats

stand over two beats
sit down over two beats
stand on **ONE** beat

(Any of these movements could be developed into whole body movements.)

27 MOVING 'IN PLACE'

Tight roll into stretch   (like an explosion)
Roll, curled up tight, then stretch out into a balance on a body part. Stress the spine stretching or arching. Pick out one child's action and all practise that one.

Body swings   (like swingboats)
side to side and forwards and back stretch high to the side then drop down deep and up the other side bend the knees, make the swing big and continuous

Stretching and bending   (like elastic)
the spine
from standing, stretch high with right hand then left
stretch to the side, forwards and backwards, downwards and upwards

Clap and stretch
clap high overhead
clap low near the ground
clap high again
lunge clap forward (front leg bent, back leg stretched)

Stretching the legs
in crouch position place the hands on the floor straighten the legs and then bend them back into crouch. Lie on the floor on the back, legs straight and together. Bend one leg and stretch it up, like a signpost. Bend it and place it on the ground again. Repeat with the other leg. Make variations of this idea.

Flopping down
stretch high, then relax through the fingertips, elbows, head, back, knees and up again at different speeds.

Shaking sequences	right foot left foot all over
Rocking	from foot to foot from side to side or forward and back, with a straight body or with a swinging body
Padding feet	stand with feet together pad from foot to foot stretching and bending the feet as much as possible
Arrow legs and arms	pull the foot into the knee and shoot it out into the space bend the arm and hand close to the body and shoot the fingers into the air make fast rhythms use all directions
Jumping	(header jumps) jump with feet together, head high (frog or star) jump from crouch position to wide in the air knee jumps with knees high turning jumps jumps off two feet onto one and vice versa (as in hopscotch)
Arm movements	swinging 'lassoing' shooting out (These can go with the above jumps.)

28 TRAVELLING ABOUT THE ROOM

Running and stopping	out of a space and back to it Run and stop. Press the back high, hands and feet on the floor (like a bridge). Run and stop. Lie down. Press toes in the air.

Flying and balancing	Run, arms outstretched. Balance on one leg. Lift the other one high.
Gallop steps	with bent knees or stretched legs, into different directions with right or left side leading
Skipping	as above
Leaping along	landing on one or two feet
Crawling	*stretching* the hand forward along the ground pulling the knee right up to the body
Sliding	along, pulling the body forwards with the arms
Wriggling	along fast
Walking (centipede)	on all fours with *straight* legs and arms bringing the feet close to the hands. This can also be done by walking the feet up to the hands and then walking the hands forward.
Marching patterns	forwards backwards sideways sequences (lifting the knees or with straight legs, pointing the feet)
These starting activities	**sitting or kneeling movements moving in place or travelling about the room**

constitute a body-training session at the beginning of the lesson. Many of the movements might arise during creative work, but the stress here is in enlivening and disciplining the body. Each movement or sequence is repeated exactly several times.

29 USING THE SPACE

Children need practice in finding a space, in distinguishing between moving in or about the room and place, and in spacing themselves in relationship to other children. Link this with any of the above ideas.

Practise:

finding a space and returning to the teacher.

travelling out of your space and *back* to it again, as if the space is 'home'.

Travelling from *one* space to *another* with skipping, galloping, creeping etc. With young or insecure children it is sometimes helpful if the children *follow* the teacher initially into new spaces using a simple travelling and stopping phrase.

exploring the space around the body. Try to use up all the space around.

30 MUSIC IN STARTING ACTIVITIES

Use music to accompany any of the ideas. One piece of music can often be used for several starting activities. Music helps to involve the body and can be interspersed with the teacher's percussion playing. However, the teacher may well find it easier not to use music at this stage when her whole attention needs to be on the children. A tambour rhythm is often more immediate and effective.

Any of the music suggested in the lessons or music index might be used. Country-dance music is useful for skipping, hopping or galloping step, combinations.

Country-dance steps might be a basis for practice in coordinating actions. Simple jazz or folk music may 'get the body going'. The teacher must decide where in the lesson music is most needed. One simple piece of music might enliven a part of the starting activities (see 48). Jazz, pop and rock music are often useful, but be aware of the restrictions imposed on dance by a repetitive beat and perpetual syncopation.

31 CHOICE OF STARTING ACTIVITY

Starting activities may not necessarily lead directly to the main part of the lesson. A contrast may sometimes be better, for example:

(a) Arrow legs and arms would be a good *linking* starting activity for 'The Icicle Garden' lesson

(b) Vigorous gallop steps and padding feet would be a good *030contrast* for the slow 'Angels' lesson.

Remember to choose a few contrasting starting activities at the beginning of each lesson. Many starting activities *could* grow into a dance if they were used *creatively* in the middle part of the lesson.

32 DIAGRAM OF STARTING ACTIVITIES

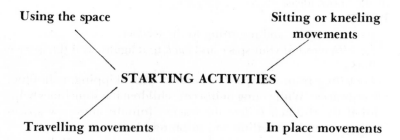

Using the space

Sitting or kneeling
movements

STARTING ACTIVITIES

Travelling movements

In place movements

Exploring and Developing Movement

33 DEVELOPMENT

This can be seen in terms of *depth* and *variety* (see **7, 21**). It involves deepening the awareness of the action, improving the child's movement response and finding other ways or variations of the movement, so that it becomes both more vivid and more varied.

This movement experience might be compared to a language experience where the child is encouraged to expand his awareness in language - 'It's an apple. It's red. It's got a rough skin. There's a hole in it. It's all crinkly on one side.' He is encouraged to 'look' more closely at an object. He is encouraged to 'feel' more vividly in movement.

34 IMPROVEMENT

It is very important to improve the performance of the child's response. This can be done in a sensitive way using praise and encouragement while expecting high standards of effort. Too often children are asked to 'explore' in a multitude of ways and never given time to become really rhythmically involved in one way. The improvement might be of an action suggested by the teacher or one initiated by the child, and include, for example:

improving the rhythm and flow of the movement
improving the use of the body parts in the action
improving the quality of the movement (see **10**).

Above all, stress that the whole body must be involved in the movement.

Improving dodging:
'Can you move your feet really quickly?
Dodge, dodge, dodge, stop.'
Improving floating:
'Are your fingers moving in the air very lightly?'
'Make your head float gently.'
Improving jumping:
'Stretch your feet.'
'Make it clear what shape you are in the air.'

Accompaniment and improvement
The quality of the action and the performance of it can be greatly

enhanced by the children sitting and *listening* to the accompaniment. For example:

  (a) Indian-bells accompaniment
  'Can you move as softly as this? Move carefully.'
  (b) A tambour accompaniment
  'Listen to the loud accent in the rhythm. Can you make your leap fit in?'

35 VARIATIONS

From any action-word idea, any number of movements may grow.

Walking variations
Walking can be performed forwards, backwards, sideways, very fast or slowly, smoothly or erratically. *Walking* can be by oneself or with a partner. We usually walk on our whole foot but we can also walk on different parts of the foot and on different parts of the body: on the heels, knees and hands etc.

All of these ways give different expressions in movement. Remember that creativity in movement is not a cataloguing of possibilities but the *growth* of movement ideas, the growth of one movement to the next. The child's variation is his own way of interpreting an idea. This does not mean that the movement has never been done before, but that his particular movement is personal to him. Creativity is possible within very small limits.

There is a moment when absorption in the movement and in the limitation provided produce a fusion between the given ideas and the child's unique response to them. He begins to create *his* sequence, to feel his own rhythm. His whole body will be involved. There will be an absorption in his face and a tenacity about his practice. Such absorption does not come immediately, but the right conditions will help it to grow.

36 QUESTIONS AND TASKS

Teachers can develop variations by asking questions on the movement and giving tasks. Questions offer choices and stimulate individual response. Tasks will encourage improving the movement and give examples of ways of moving. Remember that questions and tasks can be about:

  the body
  the quality of movement
  the space
  the relationship.

'Walking' was cited as an easily-understood action. Any other action can be varied in similar ways.

Examples of questions and tasks

What?   'Show me a "header" jump with the head going really high. What other part could go high?'
'What do your arms do as you turn?
'What do you look like (shape) as you stop?'

How?   'Crawl really slowly stretching your arms and legs.'
'Are you falling slowly or quickly?'
'Can you show me three strong arm positions?'

Where?   'Where are your hands as you stop?'
'Show me dodging forward and stop.'
'Which way (direction) are you going to skip?'

Questions and tasks can be varied endlessly. Some tasks offer more freedom of choice than others, for example: 'Listen to the rhythm. Show me what your feet do—what can your feet do to this rhythm?' or, 'Try three stamps and a leap. Ready . . .!' Both tasks have plenty of scope for creativity.

Try to keep a balance between improving and varying. Never over-develop one movement idea beyond the concentration and interest of the children.

37 OBSERVATION

It is partly through her knowledge of movement and partly through her observation of the child's response, that the teacher's facility for developing movement ideas increases. Observation can be the starting point for variation or improvement, for example: if the arms are uninvolved the teacher and children can think what the arms could be doing, and practise the ideas.

The movements of one child can be noted and the ideas shared with the rest of the class, who can all practise them, with a common rhythm following the teacher's accompaniment.

This is especially helpful for a child with poor movement ability.

Try to select *movement* ideas from observing the children. This is more encouraging to creativity than merely noting that a particular child's movement is 'good'. Encourage phrases and rhythms that come from the children. Encourage them to be aware of their own movements. There comes a time when children are ready to repeat and select in some depth, but beware of forcing this at too early an age.

The Dance

38 SELECTING IDEAS

From the movement experiences of the lesson some are selected, a beginning is chosen and an end is created (see 21). A dance is made, however, impromptu. The degree of selection and skill will vary according to the age and ability of the children. In the example lessons (Part 3), indications are given of the sort of dance which might arise from the initial actions. There are no rules about this. The dance is the result of the interaction between the movement, the teacher and the children.

The essence of the dance can usually be remembered and repeated another time. The dance might be developed or added to. Older children may recapture exact phrases, others will remake and re-explore. Very young children do not seem to need this end-product in the same way. What matters to them is the flow and delight of the movement experience.

In essence there are as many forms of dance as there are imagination to make them, but a few practical frameworks can be useful.

39 A TEACHER AND CLASS DANCE

Here the choice can be between dancing near to the teacher or away from her, back to her, around her.

For example, the children dance near the teacher, bouncing and clapping. She sends them off into the space where they dance on their 'own spot'. She brings them back to her and the dance ends with the shared action of turning, arriving low and then remaining still.

Being 'near or far' from the teacher and 'doing the same or different' is a useful format for an infant dance, where the children need the security of the teacher's proximity. The children are guided by the teacher and fun can be had in the sending away and the coming back.

40 A PARTNER DANCE

In the early stages this can be simply dancing *near* the partner. Suggest 'fitting in' together, beginning and ending together. Body shapes can clarify the beginning and ending.

Other variations involve: doing the same *action* or different; *where* they go—up, down, towards, away or following their partner; *when* they move—at the same time or one after the other.

24

Encourage them to watch each other, to make their movement relationship clear. These suggestions can be practised separately. Other ways will arise from a variety of dance situations. All kinds of expressions arise (copying, agreeing, sharing, friendly, antagonistic) when dancing *with* someone.

41 A SMALL GROUP DANCE

Small groups of children can work in a similar way. Working within a group is demanding both in movement control and socially. The action content must be *simpler* than when working individually. Young or inexperienced children will tend to lose movement quality if groupwork is demanded of them too early.

Groups might: intermingle using similar actions; dance towards, away or round the centre; change the shape of the group by coming close together, making a file or a circle; move together with other groups or one after the other.

42 AN INDIVIDUAL DANCE

This can be made at all levels of ability. The length and complexity will vary accordingly. The individual dance can be a short sequence or a more extended composition where a degree of repetition and selection have resulted in a fixed form. The dance is the individual's. He knows how it begins, grows and ends.

43 A FOLLOW-MY-LEADER DANCE

In pairs or small groups, the dance may be built on a particular formation. The file might use an action which was particularly enjoyed in the lesson. Quick observation and response is needed. The leader must be sensitive to the children following.

The leader can be changed so that each child has a chance to lead and respond. Do not expect too much movement quality when 'following' is the main requirement.

44 A CIRCLE DANCE

A circle dance can be used during the lesson tasks and in the making of a dance. A circle is a secure framework for movement. Teach the children to make a circle quickly, to move in the circle skilfully.

The children can dance: around in a circle; into the middle and out; across the middle to change places; making the circle grow larger, smaller.

45 HALF-THE-CLASS DANCE

A circle formation is a useful form for:
half the class moving around (X)
half the class sitting in the centre (O)
half the class dancing (X)
half the class making accompaniment sounds (O)

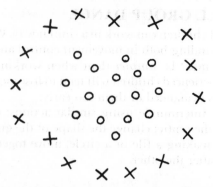

In addition, half the class may sit by the teacher and half the class dance:

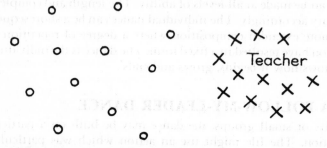

or, half the children stand 'statues' while the other half travel amongst them.

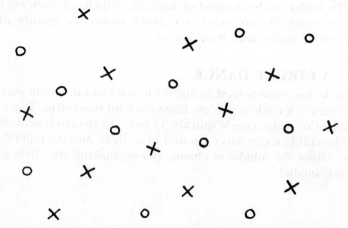

Accompaniment

The importance of accompaniment in the lesson has already been stressed in **8** and **9**. Any examples and tasks must be clearly accompanied.

46 UNACCOMPANIED MOVEMENT

When the children are asked to explore and find their own variations, they must at some point do so, without accompaniment. During this practice time, which may be very short, the teacher moves about amongst the children, encouraging them and giving occasional accompaniment help to individuals or groups. It is useful to give a time span for this practice, for example, 'When I tap on the tambour you begin. When I tap again, you stop.' In this way they learn to develop their own movement rhythms.

47 MUSIC AS ACCOMPANIMENT

Music can be a wonderful stimulus for enlivening the body (see **30**), although other forms of accompaniment are often simpler and evoke more immediate responses.

Choose music with care. Remember that the dance is *using* the music and that it is the development of the movement that must be stressed. Music can help the development of the movement idea, but music alone will not *provide* the movement ideas.

Choose pieces which are rhythmically simple or have a very clear mood content. Symphonic movements or heavily-orchestrated pieces where the phrasing is uneven are not usually suitable for children's dance.

Music for dance can be divided into the following simple categories:

1 *Rhythmic fast tempo* (accented or smooth) for jumping, stamping, clapping, turning, skipping, shooting upwards etc.

2 *Rhythmic slow tempo* (accented or smooth) for opening, closing, swaying, creeping, stretching, rising, twisting, pressing etc.

3 *Mood music*, where an atmosphere of sadness, gaiety, business, strangeness might evolve from the music. Here music can form a background for action, the movement relating to the mood and occasional accents in the music. For example, a group of children made a dance about strangely-shaped, slow-moving creatures on the moon. Electronic music was later played as a background to the movement. Sudden accents in movement

were related to sudden accents in the music. Here 'how' the children moved, i.e. slowly and carefully, was echoed by the slow, strange quality of the music, but the rhythm of the movement came from the nature of the actions.

48   MUSIC AND THE LESSON PLAN

The same piece of music can often be used for one of the starting activities as well as the dance. Percussion and voice might be used in the development part of the lesson as in 'Skipping dance Lesson'. Alternatively, music may be played at the end of the lesson to link with ideas experienced during the lesson, (as in 'Procession' and 'Action Dance to Music').

A few music suggestions are given in the lessons, and a short list of suitable music may be found in the Appendix.

A cassette of specially-composed electronic music is available with this book. The short pieces can be used with starting activities and the lessons.

Encourage the children to listen, to notice the phrasing. Some may have a strong rhythmic sense and naturally dance in time, but it is much more important for them to sense the spirit of the music and use those same qualities in the movement (see also **30**).

49   SELF-ACCOMPANIMENT WITH VOICE SOUNDS

Here the children themselves make sound and movement together. If children make sounds as they move, the rhythm and quality of the movement are strengthened.

Introduce the idea gradually. Suggest that the children use voice accompaniment in a tiny part of the lesson. Always link making a sound to making a movement. Sound and movement can be clarified simultaneously. Encourage sensitive interaction between sound and movement by such tasks as:

'Make your sound fit your action.'

'Make your sound stop when you do.'

'Sit on the floor and imagine your sound and your movement.'

Voice sounds may be linked with the actions of:

   growing slowly

   leaping

   turning

   jerking

   falling.

50 CONDUCTING VOICE SOUNDS

The children sit in front of the teacher. The teacher 'conducts' sounds The teacher performs the action with her hands. She makes her hands move and stop. The children make a sound for the action, for example humming or explosive syllables. The sound must mirror the action and stop when the hands stop.

The teacher's hands:
open and close slowly
rise high and sink with a wave-like motion
shoot upwards
flop and flop.

The sounds could be tape recorded (see **189**). In these ways the teacher guides sound and movement making, Children can move as they make sounds or observe and accompany each other.

51 ACCOMPANYING A PARTNER

This idea can be developed into partner work. One child moves while his partner accompanies him. This should be done with a very simple action phrase (use the above examples), making sure once again that there is a beginning and an ending to the movement.

In the same way voice sound can be added to, or grow with, a group composition.

Sounds used as accompaniment might equally well stimulate movement and vice versa.

For simplicity's sake, sound as a stimulus is included in Part 2.

Stimuli (general)

52 RELATING MOVEMENT TO THE WORLD AROUND US

As indicated in Part 1, movement alone, its action and rhythm can be the content of a dance. The movement can equally well be related to feelings, experiences and activities in the world around us. Classroom activities, projects, writing or artwork may give rise to movement ideas. There is a natural interplay between movement and ideas. Movement relates fundamentally to so many activities that it can be a unifying element in education. (See Index for lists of stimuli.)

53 ENCOURAGING CHILDREN'S OBSERVATION

Children can be encouraged to see, feel and hear movement in the world around them: to see the shapes of buildings, the flight of a bird, to feel the softness of fur or watch the flurrying movement of leaves caught in the wind. All these can be experienced as movement sensations and the child's sensitivity and response to everything around him developed.

54 EVALUATING THE STIMULUS

The teacher must evaluate the stimulus. Is it one which suggests a variety of action ideas? Do the latter contain contrast? Can they be developed? If the stress is on movement development, the stimulus is a *starting point* which can be referred back to, but does not have to dominate and perhaps limit the movement ideas. The stimulus should not be slavishly copied but used as fertile ground for the *selection* of ideas. Above all the stimulus should relate to the *child's experience*.

Try using different stimuli and approaches to movement with children. Compare their responses in different situations. Remember that it is the *movement content* of the lesson which must capture the attention and excite the response.

Younger children, particularly, respond far more readily to *tactile* or *visual* stimuli where they do not have to make the mental association of image to movement. Use the senses—looking, listening and touching—as much as possible.

55 IMAGERY TO REINFORCE MOVEMENT

Imagery can enrich a movement experience by adding an imaginative framework to a movement idea. Use imagery incidentally throughout the lesson, so that movement is communicated more clearly through phrases such as:

'As if you were walking on eggshells'

'Lasso arms' or

'Snake-like movement'.

Using colourful language to help broaden movement sensation and understanding, the teacher can find images relevant to the movement and experience of her class. Adults have a far larger and more sophisticated store of images than children, whose different cultures and background must also be considered.

In the above example, imagery is used to *reinforce* movement ideas. Many such images will occur to the teacher on the spur of the moment. Imagery can also suggest or stimulate movement.

56 IMAGERY AS A STIMULUS

Here the image is used as a stimulus for a variety of movement ideas. Obviously anything can be imagined. Generally speaking, the older the child, the more imagery *can* be used to provoke a quick movement response. There is little point in using images unless the child understands and is excited by them. Select action words from the image as movement starting points (see **184**). Decide whether the image alone is a sufficient stimulus or whether it needs reinforcing with pictures, objects or music etc.

57 MOVEMENT TO IMAGERY

While it is stimulating to take an image as a movement stimulus, it is also worthwhile to work the other way round—for *movement* to suggest ideas to the children. This encourages individual associations of movement to images, and often results in very original ideas (see **236**). Even if the teacher *has* decided on using a particular image, it is often a good idea to explore the movement *before* mentioning the image. For example, a lesson on witches might be more effective if lots of witch-like movements were explored and *then* the children were asked to connect the idea of 'witch' to the movement, and make their own dances.

Any of the images in the Lessons in Part 3 could be used earlier or later in the lesson.

Note too that a particular basic movement might have any number of movement associations. For example, twisting slowly might relate to the movement of a cat, genie, agony, smoke (see also 180).

Flash Cards

58 'MOVING WORDS'

Flash cards of action words have proved a good movement stimulus. They capture attention and provoke an immediate movement response. Obviously the words must relate to the child's experience both in movement and reading. The development of language and movement skills can be closely linked, and the use of flash cards can reinforce both these skills.

Write the 'moving words' on large, brightly-coloured cards. Hold a card up. Ask the children to, 'Dance the word. Don't tell me. Show me!' and then quickly provide a simple rhythmic accompaniment to keep the movement going, and improve the quality of the movement. Many of the Lessons could include the use of flash cards

59 WORD 'MESSAGES'

(See Action Words 11.) Flash cards can be held up as 'messages'.

Stretch Flop
Spin

Children dance the message. They can take it in turns to hold up the message. The emphasis must be on the many ways they 'say' their message in movement. Can they make the message interesting to watch? Then groups can each be given a 'secret' message. Each group has to guess the other groups' messages.

('Messages' can also be interpreted through movement with sounds—see **228**.)

60 PAIR WORDS

Hold up two contrasting words and ask the children to link them together in movement—to 'join them up'. Seize upon the initial response and use accompaniment to enlarge and clarify the movement. Partner work could follow. Partners could dance in unison, for example turning and jumping together, or one child might dance *jumping*, the other child dance *turning*.

Partner relationships, around each other, or beside each other, help the idea to grow into a partner dance.

61 PLACEMENT OF CARDS

The words might equally well be written on a *blackboard* or on a large sheet of *paper*. Then the action word can be *pointed* at, rather than held up.

If children are organized to dance group by group, flash cards can be placed on the floor. Children dance beside the word and then move on to another. Encourage them to use as many ideas as possible, to make a dance moving around the word.

Think of other ways of using cards. Use ideas involving: guessing; choosing; communicating etc.

62 LANGUAGE—MOVEMENT GAMES

In the classroom, movement might well be an aid to understanding and enjoying language. In the dance lesson, language stimulates movement, and it is the full *enactment* and *rhythm* of the latter which is of paramount importance. It is the immediacy of words to movement that is enjoyed.

63 WORDS AS PATTERNS

When the children are familiar with the words they enjoy word patterns which 'look like' the action they represent.

64 A STRETCH CARD

A ten-foot-long 'stretch' card once delighted a group of children. They said the word as they stretched into elongated shapes. They also used the card as an object to stretch—stride along *beside* and stretch—jump over.

The idea grew into a *dance* when the action of rolling arose—because the card kept on rolling up! Stretching and rolling sequences developed. The card then became a cylindrical *enclosure*. Four children at a time crouched inside, stretched up, jumped out and stretched and rolled away.

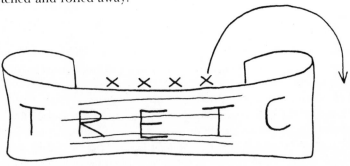

Flash cards can be made by the teacher or the children and can arise from any classroom activity or topic. Any action words or combinations of words used in the 'Lessons' are suitable. Unusual or colourful words arising from poems or topics might be explored in movement.

65 NOUNS AND ADJECTIVES

These can also be used on flash cards. Here the word or image has to be 'translated' into action.

Challenge the children to, 'Show me what you think of doing to this idea.' The word on the card is the stimulus for several action ideas.

Pliable EXPANSION

Escape

One method is to place these around on the floor near the end of the lesson. Each child chooses one and 'moves' the idea. Subsequent lessons might select one favourite image or partner/group work can result from a variety.

Encourage a quick movement response to the word. Do not develop variations but help each child to clarify his response. Parners might work on passing on their movement' (i.e. copying each other, see 181-8).

Movement Patterns

66 DRAWING A DESIGN

Many actions can be communicated through drawing simple designs. This stimulus has been particularly effective where the children lack concentration and listening ability, or have language difficulties.

If the teacher draws the design with vivid colours on a large piece of paper *during* the dance lesson, the response is always very lively. The teacher draws, the children watch, then, without speaking, dance the design. Suggest to the children: 'Watch the movement design. What is it doing? Can you show me the movement?' Be ready to help with movement suggestions to encourage and develop the response.

Draw bouncing, zig-zag, twisting or sliding patterns.

The size, quality and rhythm of the movement can be shown in the drawings. The movement communication is therefore very vivid, as in the following suggestions:

1 Draw a *large* twisting pattern.
2 Draw a large twisting pattern very *strongly*.
3 Draw it very *slowly* or *fast*.

Suggest the arms and hands lead the movement, then the foot or the elbow. Help them discover the changes of shape as the body moves.

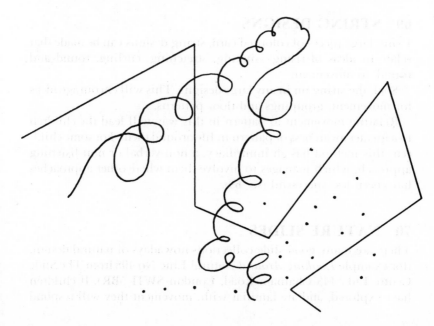

67 USING CHILDREN'S DESIGNS

Making designs with paint or collage might well be a follow-up to a movement lesson and in turn stimulate dance ideas. Lesson **191** is an example of this. Words, movement and design are interrelated.

One teacher *combined* design making and dance within one lesson. A long strip of paper was placed down the centre of the room. The children each had their *drawing* space (kneeling by the paper) and their *moving* space. The method was to move (e.g. spin and stop) and then draw, trying to use the same *quality*, i.e. light, strong, large, in the drawing as in the movement.

Coloured chalks and fat pens were used. Afterwards the design was worked on and a long vivid pattern produced. The pattern was then the stimulus for a subsequent lesson. Obviously careful selection of *movement* ideas is needed.

68 DESIGN FOR AN OVERHEAD PROJECTOR

Other children have drawn simple designs for an overhead projector and their designs have then been projected and used as a dance stimulus. Care must be taken that the patterns and designs are given due importance, and that they become colourful works in their own right, not mere representations of movement.

69 STRING DESIGNS

Using large pieces of coloured card, string designs can be made that relate to ideas of rising—sinking, stretching, curling, round and round, to movement.

Stick the string on in any large designs, This will encourage ideas for movement, groupings and floor patterns.

Relating movement to pattern in this way will lead the children to a greater awareness of pattern in life around them. For some children, this method has an immediacy, a non-verbal or non-listening approach, which manages to involve them where other approaches have been less successful (see **69**).

70 NATURE SLIDES

There are many good slide collections nowadays of natural design, (for example *Looking Around* Natural Line No 498 from The Slide Centre Ltd., 143 Chatham Road, London SW11 5BR). If children have explored, and are familiar with, movement they will respond well to such stimuli. Their movement experience relates to what they *see*.

Similarly, designs from nature photography such as *Shells in Colour*, published by Penguin Books, offer good stimuli. The shells also have beautiful names, such as Star Turrids, Pteropods, the Threaded Wentletrap, which might give ideas for moving and also be used as accompaniments (see also **112**).

The most effective teaching method, after a vigorous warm-up, is (as with the objects or flash cards) to ask the children to *look* at the stimuli and then move immediately without talking, into a movement or a body shape. The moving in silence brings about a concentration on an idea, however slight. The children need to show their idea in *movement*, not words. Action words then help to clarify the response, for example, 'I liked that rolling along very small, then enlarging the movement into a sharp shape.' After this initial work the children will also respond readily to patterns in modern paintings (see **189-91**).

Objects

71 MOVING THINGS

Things that move, or can be moved, are invaluable in quickly involving children and suggesting ways of moving. Words alone are often not enough. Young children only need to *watch* intently and with the empathy towards things very evident in young children they will quickly respond in movement. Teachers who have classes with language problems find this approach useful. Language and movement can be extended simultaneously. Small, easily-managed objects are most suitable.

72 A LIST OF THINGS TO WATCH

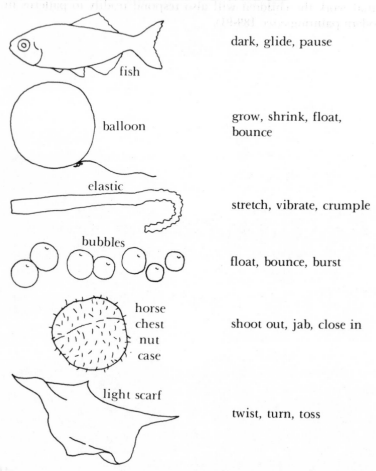

fish	dark, glide, pause
balloon	grow, shrink, float, bounce
elastic	stretch, vibrate, crumple
bubbles	float, bounce, burst
horse chest nut case	shoot out, jab, close in
light scarf	twist, turn, toss

Some of these can be handled so that sensitivity to their quality increases. Very often the shape of the object will suggest starting and ending positions. Remember that the movement can always be experienced in a part of the body as well as in whole body movements. For example, a fish movement can be expressed by hands darting and gliding in the space around the body. Then the whole body gliding into a new space.

Many things do not 'do' anything, but action words can be linked with them. For example, a rock suggests: pressing strongly into different shapes rolling and balancing (see also 114).

73 OBJECTS WITH SOUNDS

Sometimes the chosen object will make a sound as it moves, and then there is a double stimulus of suggested movement and a given phrase of sound. Elastic 'pings' back to size. Children can 'grow' to the sound of the teacher (or their partner) 'blowing them up'; a top has a humming sound. Appropriate voice sounds can be added to the movement by the teacher or the children. If making the sound seems only to distract the children instead of helping the movement quality, they probably are not ready to combine movement and sound (see Voice Sound Accompaniment 49).

Dividing up the class

It is possible to divide the different movement elements of the object between the class, for example: balloon; half grow, balance and crumple; half float gently amongst them.

74 GREEN CELLOPHANE

Often the simplest things can stimulate movement ideas. A small piece of green cellophane attracted one group of children. They watched it float downwards. It zig-zagged down. It slid along the floor. It could be screwed up and gradually opened out again.

75 SMALL TOYS

These have been most useful because of the simplicity of their movement:

a soft floppy animal
rag doll
spinning top

small rocking horse
ball
cotton-reel snake
A variety of action words arise:
flop
spin
rock
collapse
balance
jerk.

The teacher can ask, 'What does it do? (Make it move.) Can you do that?' and give the children a chance to answer in movement. Then the focus must be on the children's response and its development. There is little value in just copying exactly what the thing does.

Action words can help to define the movement. The actions can be practised singly, then in simple combinations, or the movement might be varied by practising the action with different body parts and different body shapes (see **198** and **195**).

Of course, all these toys could be imagined and the ideas used in a toyshop dance with a framework of: wake up, move, go back to sleep again.

But as a movement stimulus the real thing has invariably proved a stronger stimulus to experiencing basic actions and qualities of movement. Use *Listen, Move and Dance* records.

76   OBJECTS AS PROPERTIES

Different actions will arise if the objects are used as properties while dancing. The quality of the property can be echoed in the body (see, Dancing with a balloon **194**).

Dancing with a light scarf, the teacher can ask 'Where does the scarf take you—up, down, around?'

With the idea of following the scarf, the whole body will stretch, bend and twist. Coloured crêpe paper, streamers, have been used similarly in a number of dances.

In the same way, dancing with small percussion instruments will stretch the body. Ideas for infants are Smarties tubes filled with something that rattles and secured with sticky tape (see Percussion Dance **230**).

Other objects to dance with are:
chairs
cardboard boxes
cushions
dusters
newspapers
gloves
towels.

For example, a cushion
can be sat on
lifted high
pummelled
squeezed
stroked
jumped over.

A framework might be: 'pick it up. Move with it. Put it down', to a clear time span for movement.

The objects can be danced with as things or fantasy can change their nature and they become islands, enemies or magic properties.

Defining the movement
Any movement that arises can be clearly defined by thinking of the action phrase and what that consists of.

The teacher must decide whether the object is one to be *handled* and danced with, or *watched* — or a combination of the two. With less-experienced children it is generally easier to try one type of object initially—a variety in one lesson will produce more ideas than it will be possible to develop.

The following Lessons use objects: **192-202; 221** and **237**.

77 MAKING THINGS FOR YOUNG CHILDREN

When working with young children real things that move are very stimulating. Nursery and infant school teachers have made their own:
floppy dolls
beanbag frogs
rag octopus
stocking snakes
paper-bag puppets
a crêpe-paper swisher
a spinning spiral
a shape mobile

and used them with great success as movement guides and stimuli. At dance times (and with a very young child this is probably not a formal lesson) they can stimulate qualitative action and simple phrases of movement (see **238**).

78 SNAKE

'What is he doing? Yes, curling up very tight and stretching out *very* long. You do that. Ready! And curl up tight, tight and stretch out, stretch out l - o - n - g. And curl up . . .' etc.

Make the snake (a stuffed stocking) do lots of other movements that will stretch and bend the children's bodies up into the air, along the ground, from kneeling, lying or standing. 'Habanera' from *Listen Move and Dance* is a good musical accompaniment for this.

79 PAPER-BAG PUPPET

The puppet can be a character—a soldier, marching and turning, or a clown, jumping and balancing.

The children do the movement with the puppet, or the puppet can be a king or magician character who tells the children what to do. This fantasy element encourages great involvement. Children have to listen to the puppet, watch the puppet (see Lesson Shaky king **237**).

Try making a collection of home-made movement stimuli. Give them names; make them personal.

Dressing Up

80 LARGE PIECES OF CLOTH

Dressing up as a stimulus for dance can use the quality of the garment, how it affects the body's basic movement, rather than as a specific costume. Large pieces of cloth can become cloaks, camouflage or swirling skirts (see Lesson Cloaks **203**). If children dress up spontaneously in the classroom they can be asked, 'how do you move in that costume?' Try to relate it to action words. Help the other children to watch, feel the movement, practise it to a voice rhythm. Little phrases of dance may be experienced in this way. Later in a dance lesson the movement that resulted can be recaptured without necessarily wearing the costume and repeated many times so that it becomes part of the body vocabulary, such as 'Remember that really slow proud walk.' On the other hand, clothes may suggest a character, for example baggy trousers conjure up the idea of a clown.

81 MAKING COSTUMES

Simple and quickly-made costumes can be made from:
  newspaper (hats and collars)
  black dustbin bags (witches' clothes) cut head and arm holes.
  paper plates (masks see Anger **207**)
  paper bags (masks).
How to Make Masks by Michael Kingsley Skinner (Studio Vista) gives clear directions for simple mask making.

82 A BOX OF COSTUMES

The box is placed in the centre of the room. Half the class watches, while the other half moves.
One by one, each child walks to the box, takes a costume puts it on and then makes a statue in character in a space of the room.

At a given signal each child moves as his costume suggests, then stops, again in character. One by one the children replace the costumes and sit by the teacher. The accompaniment might be a drum beat or quiet background music. Many older classes have performed this exercise with great absorption. It must be done with clear moving and stopping. Discussion about the movement follows. Define it in action words. Suggest how to make the movements larger and more rhythmic.

83   LIST OF COSTUMES

Costume wearing can be initiated in the classroom or by a few children as an introduction to the idea during a lesson. The movement can be realistic or fantastic.

Costumes can suggest movement ideas, or they can be used to make an existing dance more vivid. The following costumes and ideas have arisen in the past:

shoes — a funny step rhythm. Step, step, lift (the knee), step, step, lift 'bouncing shoes' that will not stop

beret — a head-shaking, nodding, palsied creature, or a person led by their head - the head takes you high, low, around, *follow* the head

skirt — turning, rising and sinking if worn over the head - groping, stretching

scarf — swirling, whirling, leaping dance if tied round the head - a creeping, pouncing bandit dance.

Any number of ideas will arise. *Select* and develop a few or help the children to do so, so that they have some *definite* movement idea to practise.

Any such activity should not be attempted until the children have a good control of going and stopping, (see also **146**).

People

84 MOVEMENT CHARACTERS

Different types of people have different movement characteristics. In order to make a 'movement character' select action words To 'describe' that person, for example:

a strong, striding person

a pushing person

a flopping person

a dithering person.

Practise the initial action type in sequences of action, for example *a dithering person* — use small, light steps with frequent changes of direction, small, light hand and head movement, quick, light changes of position — this way, that way;

a strong person — strong, striding steps, wide-armed open turns, emphatic jumps.

Make a phrase of movement which travels, then moves in place. Repeat it many times.

Encourage the children to use contrasting qualitative movement and discover the sort of characters that emerge. Children could then develop one idea as 'their' character. This character could be given a name. Remember to guide the children to make a 'movement sentence' about their type of person.

Partner work — each character moving in turn, or *group work* — each group with a particular character (the lazy group, the happy group) might well follow.

The characters could be related to particular situations or people; for instance, school characters, family characters.

The more personal the ideas become, the more the children enjoy them. Any number of people can be depicted in movement by asking the children:

'How do they move?'

'What actions do they use?'

'What do they look like (body shape)?'

85 CLOWNS

Explore variations of walking and falling as the basic idea and make rhythmic sequences of movement, with a partner or the teacher. This emphasis is on a richness of funny ideas for walking and falling rather than mimetic clown actions. For example, walk on your heels with arms wide; turn with one leg high; fall over slowly; jump up again quickly.

Use a definite rhythm to practise the above phrases then suggest the children make their own clown walks and falls (see Clowns **204**).

86   THE 'MR MEN BOOKS' BY ROGER HARGREAVES

These are a good source of ideas for young children. Select *one* main action word to 'describe' the character and use it in a variety of ways:

Mr Jelly
jelly walks
jelly hands   jelly head
jelly shapes
jelly jumps.

87   GHOSTS

Use movement to a quiet humming accompaniment: stretching *slowly* into wide shapes at different levels. Curling quickly and vice versa, then floating and turning slowly or quickly from one spot to another.

Groups of children can dance together in threes using different shapes and levels.

Ghosts appear and disappear from and into a variety of body positions. They intermingle. The dance accelerates into a fast, light, whirling dance. A sudden stop and the ghosts vanish. (The idea of *vanishing* provokes many movement ideas.)

This particular lesson was most successful when the movements were practised before the suggested imagery which arose originally from discussion about 'Night time'. The children then had movement examples on which to base their expression of 'ghosts'. Other ideas include Witches (**206**) and Red Indians (**205**)

88   THE PIED PIPER STORY

This story can be used to show the movement of the people and the movement of the rats. One group of children did not attempt to dance the whole story. They danced selected ideas and the rest was shown by a series of paintings. The following sequences were worked on in rhythmic phrases, interspersed with showing paintings.

The Rats — hide, peep out, zig-zag
The People — dodge, jump up in the air
The Rats — follow my leader skipping, tumble and drown
The People — clapping, skipping, meeting and parting, sinking slowly and sadly down.

Moods and Emotions

89 FEELINGS

Feelings can be expressed through dance, but this is an area where the function of dance is often misunderstood.

Just to *feel* is not enough. It is the *movement expression* of the feeling that is important. Too often movement that expresses an emotion is unoriginal and unimaginative because the movement possibilities that arise from feeling have not been developed. The following examples relate movement to mood:

Anger could suggest punching, stamping, leaping and landing strongly.

Practice of single actions could develop into a sequence: two stamping steps forward, a high leap with punching arms, landing strongly (see **207** and **233**).

Sadness: slow walks to kneeling,

sinking down slowly,

rising strongly,

rocking forwards and backwards or side to side at different speeds.

Happiness: light skipping, hands clapping, small, high accent jumps, meeting and parting and dancing around a partner.

Fear, Laughter, Patience or *Impatience* can be explored similarly.

90 MOOD VOICE SOUNDS

Taped and danced, mood voice sounds have proved a good accompaniment to the above ideas. It is possible to make a collection of 'angry phrases' with the children. Make an angry word rhythm to accompany movement.

No no *no!* . . .

Go *away!* Go *away!* . . .

I won't! I won't! . . .

91 'THE GREAT BLUENESS'

This story, by Arnold Lobel, describes a town where everything is grey. The people are very tired of grey and ask the magician for help. He mixes a magic paint and everything is painted blue. Everyone is happy but then they become tired of blue. It makes them depressed. So then yellow paint is provided. Happiness . . . but then yellow hurts their eyes. Everywhere is painted red, but red makes them angry. In the end multicoloured paint is produced, using all the colours of the rainbow and everyone is happy.

Many movement ideas arise from this (compressed) story. It is so rich in possibilities that movement must be selected and planned carefully or the content will be superficially enacted.

The three moods: depressed, angry, and happy might be the stimulus
stimulus for three contrasting groups using: floppy, strong or light, quick movement qualities.

Each group could begin and end with a 'picture', frozen, contrasting body positions which come to life and move, and then return to the picture.

Depressed mood — move from standing to kneeling with a flop and sigh. And *'flop'*. Move from kneeling to sitting to half lying, or through a roll to half standing thereby creating a number of depressed positions and movements.

Alternatively the dance might be in rondo form. Make body shapes to suggest: depressed, hurt eyes, anger, interspersed with 'painting' movements.

For example, 'Hold your angry shape quite still so that you look like a picture of an angry crowd. Here comes the painting music. Show me painting on the spot, high, low and all around you — big movements.'

The moods of many stories or situations can be abstracted and developed through actions, body shapes and relationships.

One group of children danced with different coloured streamers 'painting' the air around the body with large flexible movements. 'The Great Blueness' might equally well be linked to a dance about colours.

Animals

92 'HOW DO THEY MOVE?'

Animals, real or fantastic, provide a rich source of movement ideas. The following examples indicate how movement phrases can be selected to give a dance-like rather than mimetic expression. Other animals can be similarly explored by asking, 'What do they do?', 'How do they move?', and by selecting movement which brings about exciting contrasts of action, direction or rhythm.

93 WILD HORSE

A photograph of a *free wild horse* could initiate: a free-flow high gallop and pull up, gallop and swerve, head toss into body turn, heel-tossing jumps and sudden stops, sequences of the above.

94 DOLPHINS

Dolphins leap and dive, twist in the air and dive and roll.
Children can practise leaping with their heads, knees or chests high, slow-motion diving leading to rolling, stretching or pressing upwards. Half the class could leap while the other half dives.

95 THE ZOO

A broader topic such as the Zoo requires careful selection of a few movement contrasts. Several characteristic movements might be worked on initially; then one or two favourites selected and explored in depth so that the children have a choice.
Monkeys — running on all fours, then running lightly on the feet. Four runs on all fours. Four runs on the feet.
Elephants — plodding and turning, stretching and bending the knees and ankles.
Seals — lying on the floor — arching back, stretched rolls,slithering. Develop one of the above sequences in pairs or groups by varying directions and adding actions, for example elephant head-swings and heavy rolls.

96 PRIMITIVE ANIMAL DANCES

Older children have enjoyed learning about primitive animal dances. Here the dancer becomes like the animal and imitates its movement qualities.

Certain characteristic phrases are repeated over and over again.
A deer
  ru u un, leap and swerve
  ru u un, leap and swerve.
Curt Sachs, in *World History of the Dance* vividly describes the movement of several animal dances. These descriptions reinforce ideas of selecting, repeating and rhythmicising movement so that it becomes dance. He writes of primitive man's belief: 'To imitate animals means to win power over them'; or, 'To imitate them in their distinctive characteristics means taking and rendering useful their magic power.' The 'Folk Lore of Mexico' record could be used for such ritual dances.

97 FANTASY CREATURES

The movement of imaginary creatures on another planet can be defined by the questions: 'How do they go?' 'How do they move?'

The following diagram indicates the phrases óf action which may arise from such a stimulus (see also **241**).

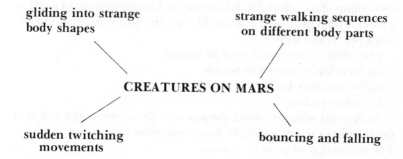

gliding into strange
body shapes

strange walking sequences
on different body parts

CREATURES ON MARS

sudden twitching
movements

bouncing and falling

98 ANIMAL NAMES AS STIMULI

Children can invent names of strange animals. There are many examples of strange animal names in poetry books and stories, such as dinosaur names, for example, Diplodocus. These might stimulate ways of moving as in the 'Mars' example above, or the words might be used as rhythms to accompany strange movement (see Chants **121** and Dinosaurs **210**). (See also **208-211**.)

Nature

Nature is a rich source of movement ideas. Select action words which arise from the movement and shapes of the stimulus.

99 WATER

Water suggests actions such as:
  running and pausing
  whirling and stopping
  splashing up
  rocking gently.
The above should be practised in phrases, coordinating different parts of the body and finding new movements. Then two actions might be linked together to form an action phrase.
  Splash *up* and *up* and *up* (getting different body parts high).
  W h i r l STOP (opening the arms).
  Practise this.
One infant class enjoyed watching the rocking movement of water in a bowl, which produced a dream-like quality in the children's movement (see Water **215**).
  The whole class might *rock* in unison
  on their knees from side to side
  curled on their backs
  from foot to foot.
As in many nature stimuli, the action of the water, or the action of the people in water, could be a starting point.
The movement of people in water
  shoot up and glide down
  open and close arms and legs
  jump down, shake up.
Each phrase could be further clarified either through tasks or creative work.
  'Start in crouch position, Shoot the fingers high and stretch. Come down gently with the palms leading.' (See Swimming pool **242**.)
  Use Water Sound from *BBC Sound Effects*.

100 VOLCANO

Stimulate the movement by photographs and word descriptions such as those contained in *Volcanoes* published by HMSO. Use percussion accompaniment made by the children themselves (rumbling drum-beats, sudden accents) and perhaps tape-recorded. Discuss the movement ideas beforehand and have clear starting points in the lesson. Alternatively, use the image for the first time in a dance lesson, for the sake of the dance experience, and also to stimulate interest in volcanoes. Use the images of:

lava - slowly rolling and spreading
rocks - exploding upwards
smoke - curling, swirling.

A dramatic effect is achieved if the children are free to decide when the explode upwards. Everyone has a slow turning preparation and then leaps upwards, all at different times. Small groups can explode one after the other. Body shapes in the air and on the ground can be clarified.

The action of people running, dodging and stopping provides other action themes.

Choose two contrasting ideas to work on in the lesson and divide them between groups or partners.

101 FIRE

Similarly fire can be explored by means of the words: writhe, twist and shoot.

Fire movement such as writhing, could begin in one part of the body and spread to other body parts, or begin with one child and spread to others.

Suggestions such as, 'Show me different parts of yourself shooting out like flames as I play the instrument', stimulate movement variety.

The dance could be done in a circle, the outer group writhing and twisting, the inner shooting out flames! One teacher brought in strips of red crêpe paper for the children to whirl and move with. 'The Fire of London' as a topic might relate very well to dance in this way.

102 OTHER NATURE SUGGESTIONS

Other useful titles under Nature include:

Wind (see **217**)
River
Reflections
Rocks (**222**)
Birds (**212**)
Storm (**217**)

Desert
Flowers (see Seasonal events **110**)
Oil wells.

When planning the idea it is helpful to jot down the movement possibilities and then select one or two. There is a danger with stimuli of trying to cover too many ideas so that no in-depth work is achieved. Older children will respond well to nature stimuli if these are put within very clearly-defined frameworks, particularly where relationships are stressed.

103   MIRAGE

'Mirage' from the Desert image initiated slow, light changes of level and shape within a group. A leader was chosen and the rest 'fitted in' with his movements, opening, closing, rising, sinking. Different group shapes emerged, melted away and reformed.

Use slow music from BBC Radiophonic Music (see **212-217**).

Seasonal Events

Seasonal events and rituals are frequently used as topics for project work in schools and provide a rich source of ideas for dance (see also 144).

104 CHRISTMAS

This is traditionally the time of the mime and the tableau, but Christmas dances using simple combinations of actions and step patterns are easy to evolve.

Decide upon the character or event that is to be portrayed. Select an action, word or short phrase as a starting point for movement development. Remember that dance is not miming events but communicating the qualities and rhythms embodied within the situation.

For example, *The Crowd in Bethlehem* was a starting point. People were hurrying to find somewhere to sleep. The action of 'hurrying' was selected. The movement tasks were:

1   hurrying and pausing (to a given drum beat with lots of short phrases)
2   hurrying and pausing, changing direction
3   hurrying and pausing, changing direction and avoiding people
4   beginning with hurrying and then *slowing* down to walking heavily (practised many times to a regularly repeated rhythm)
5   sinking down to the ground slowly (tired), resting on one knee, or two, in different positions
6   choosing when to hurry, when to pause, when to avoid, when to slow down, when to rest in a position.

The above example indicates the movement detail and repetition involved if the movement is to be clear and fully experienced. It is important to repeat each phrase many times so that a rhythmic flow is developed, for example hurry, hurry, hurry, hurry, hurry, slow down, slow down and sink down and still. Use voice and tambour to give a clear phrase.

Shepherds can open and close the body (use imagery of stretching and looking out over the fields) from a variety of starting positions. Use: run and look, close up tight and look or, open wide and look (as Gabriel appears).

Accompaniment

Use percussion instruments for background sound, with tambours and woodblocks playing muted 'hurrying' rhythms for the crowd idea, or to accompany the rhythm of the movement. (Angels are exemplified in **218**; Stars in **221**.)

105 CAROLS

Carols of different moods and rhythms have proved good accompaniments. Generally speaking, use the melodies and rhythms rather than the sense of the words, such as 'Patapan' for a jumping, skipping, turning step pattern to express 'Rejoicing'.

Ideas from the children are of course most valuable. A group of older juniors suggested Christmas titles such as:

Candles — rising, sinking, turning in files or circles carrying candles.

Meeting friends — in groups of four: each child dances with each of others; all four dance together.

Christmas presents — coming alive

Mobiles — swaying.

106 GUY FAWKES

Use action ideas such as Rockets — shooting up and sinking down; Catherine wheels — whirling around or whirling parts of the body; Crackerjacks — sudden small jumps and stops.

The rhythmic accompaniment is important. Give clear models and tasks, for example:

Crackerjacks

    hop, hop, hop, *jump* (onto two feet)

    hop, hop, hop, *jump*.

Remember that any action can be the basis of individual or group work.

Older children enjoyed making a rocket group shape using different levels and pointing a variety of body parts in one direction. They began swaying gently and built the sway into a crescendo which leapt them skywards. They sank gently down into different shapes at the end. This was practised many times over.

Use 'Troyte' from *Enigma Variations* by Elgar, or percussion (see **219**).

107 WINTER

Ideas for winter include:

1 *Ice*

freezing and melting (stretching into shapes and flopping).

ice groups forming, travelling and reforming

Use *Atmospheric Sound Effects* (BBC REC 225) (See also 220.)

2 *Keeping warm*

stamping jumps alternating with swinging, beating arms.

With jumping and swinging as an initial limitation all sorts of interesting movement combinations can arise.

Use lively music to accompany, such as 'The Wellington Boot Dance' from *John Peel's Archive Things* REC 68 M.

The Snowy Day by Ezra Jack Keats (Picture Puffin) contains many 'snowy day' ideas. Select and rhythmicize action words.

108 HALLOWEEN

Suggestions include:

witches

night rides

or magic

(See Witches 206 and the section Magic 142.)

This topic is an exciting one. It is important to select a small number of movement starting points and *develop* them. Use voice chants or music to accompany, for example Falla's *Ritual Fire Dance* or Mussorgsky's *Night on the Bare Mountain*. (See Dressing up 81 and 160.)

109 HARVEST TIME

The work action connected with harvest time can be linked in rhythmic phrases: throw, throw, throw and rise (throwing seed); cut and cut and cut and rest (scything);

stoop and lift and walk, walk, stoop and . . . (gathering).

Accompaniment might be a harvest song. Groups of children could dance different phrases.

Alternatively the movements of wheat — growing, swaying, collapsing — could result in a more abstract dance of individuals or small groups.One school produced a dance where these movements were performed simultaneously: within the dance, growing, swaying and collapsing were continually happening in different rhythms and group patterns.

Once again the above example would only be used if it was connected with the children's own experience, such as through
discussion of harvest time in different countries. Harvesting might
equally well stimulate a dance about the movement of machinery!

110 SPRING AND EASTER

The ideas embodied in the image of spring may be explored in a
similar way. The poem 'Springburst' in *There's Motion Everywhere*
by John Travers Moore, has been used for a theme on 'Growing'.

Ask the children for spring words (growing, opening, pushing,
scattering) and make a spring dance.

Use a short extract from the beginning of Debussy's 'Printemps' for
opening, closing and turning flowers. Fade the music and play a gay
rhythm on a tambourine for a happy spring dance (see 114).

A spring project could be combined with an *Easter egg dance*, the
Easter egg being the cardboard sort that has presents inside.

Half the class sits in a large, egg shaped circle. The other half
crouches inside the circle and 'comes alive' as different kinds of toys.
Perhaps the circle could be linked with a brightly-coloured ribbon.
The children hold the ribbon and move gently up and down before
the presents wake up. (See 75.)

111 CLASS WALKS

Class walks can have a dual purpose of collecting natural objects
(leaves, flowers etc.) and observing movement. On returning, stick on
or draw on a huge sheet of paper anything collected or seen. Write
movement words near them. Very often the movement seen on the
walk offers immediate stimulus for movement. For example, gulls
circling and pausing or a piece of paper lifting and dropping in the
wind.

Again, remember that these experiences are starting points. It is the
development which makes the movement absorbing. For example,
one group noticed a couple walking arm in arm. This was a starting
point for the following movement: face each other. Link opposite
arms. Do eight skips round and eight skips back. Then the children
experimented with different ways of linking arms: two hands, one
hand, back to back, holding two hands, shoulder grips, and
combinations with different directions and steps.

For further ideas, read chapter 12, 'The children's calendar', from
Opie's *The Lore and Language of Schoolchildren* and *Festivals* by
Ruth Manning Sanders (see also 119 and 212-217).

Shapes and Sculpture

112 NATURAL SHAPES

Visits to exhibitions of sculpture may spark off movement ideas. In addition, the natural shapes in the environment give ideas for: body shapes,actions and relationships between people. As a movement framework, suggest the children move from one shape to another.

Ideas that emerge from looking at shapes may result in fantasy situations, for example where the shapes 'become' types of creatures (see **97**). The shapes may relate to mood or may stimulate abstract dance where there is no meaning besides that of patterns and rhythms. In any ideas using shapes it is important to stress movement continuity, shapes evolving out of moving rather than a meaningless series of poses.

113 A TWISTED TWIG

A large twisted twig suggested the actions of twisting and pausing. Two children began apart from each other and travelled with twisting arm and leg gestures towards each other. They met and one 'led' the other into twisted shapes. This accelerated and grew stronger, twisting, turning, moving up and down until they jumped apart and rolled away into stillness. Their next idea was for one to 'grow' into a twisted shape while the other leapt and turned around her.

114 A LIST OF IDEAS

Ideas which have started exploratory work on moving shapes include:
  a mobile
  a clay model
  pebbles
  sea shells
  photographs of sculpture
  parts of an engine.

Looking at stones
Translate the shape of the stones into body shapes. Work with a partner. Make smooth, knobbly or long shapes. Make interlocking groups placing yourself under, over or between other children (see **222**).

Flowers

Use the design of the flower: groups opening and closing to the centre; groups sitting or lying with their feet to the centre.

115 MAKING SCULPTURES

Children Make Sculpture by Elizabth Leyh (Van Nostrand Reinhold) has beautiful photographs of natural and child-made sculpture. Dance work can be linked with making shapes and designs in clay, wood and wire.

Sound

116 PERCUSSION INSTRUMENTS

As well as accompanying movement (**9**), percussion instruments can be used as a stimulus for movement. The different sounds can imitate different ways of moving, using different body parts and speeds.

A cymbal suggests smooth turns, smooth travelling and arm movements, sudden leaps, sudden falls vibrating, and collapsing. The shape of the cymbal could also be used to suggest group shapes or floor patterns.

Clappers suggest fast dodging from side to side, jerking movements and flopping.

Suggestions for ways of moving can come from the teacher and children. A lesson might be based on two contrasting movements (see Adventure **236**).

Experiment with playing instruments in different ways. Encourage interest in listening to and making sounds. Link with music lessons. Make group percussion pieces by combining and repeating sounds. Remember the percussion can stimulate action, accompany the action and be danced with. (See Percussion dance or use *Listen Move and Dance* No. 4 HMV CLP 3531.)

117 HOMEMADE INSTRUMENTS AND SOUND EFFECTS

Interesting sounds can be produced by beating, shaking or tapping anything that might produce a sound such as:

knocking pebbles together — pebble rhythms
tapping a stick on the floor
beating a saucepan
screwing up newspaper
shaking a homemade shaker
hitting wooden spoons together.

These instruments could all be danced with and played simultaneously.

118 PEBBLE SOUNDS

Tap them high, low and all around the body.
Make up-and-down, and side-to-side rhythms.
Tap them quickly while *running* and *turning*.
Tap them high in the air while leaping.

Make a partner dance. One child dances with the pebbles around the other child kneeling. Change over.

119 NEWSPAPER SOUNDS

Screw the newspaper up with big, twisting movements.
Make the crackling sound start and stop.
Shake a sheet of newspaper.
Make *whipping* sounds and movement with a strip of newspaper.
Using big movements, slowly fold up a sheet of newspaper. Try
   not to make a sound (see also **200.**)
Make an individual dance. Begin it by sitting quite still on a piece of newspaper. Tape record 'newspaper sounds' as a background accompaniment.

   Remember: to explore the movement in disciplined phrases of action. Each idea must be repeated many times. Sometimes the movement may remind the children of a particular mood or experience and this may be incorporated in the dance.
The Musical Instrument Recipe Book contains details for making instruments. The record *BBC Sound Effects Sampler* No.3 contains sound effects from life around, such as 'Ping Pong'; 'Surf'. (See **216.**)

120 BODY CONTACT SOUNDS

These include:
   clicking fingers
   clapping hands
   slapping the body
   stamping on the floor
   tapping on the floor
   smoothing the floor
   rubbing the hands together.
Use one activity at a time to begin with — perhaps slapping or tapping rhythms. Stress silence and stillness at the beginning and end of each sound. Then encourage the children to *move* with the sound. Interesting sequences will arise if they then work on linking sounds and movements, such as a stamping, clapping dance or a slapping, leaping dance.
Mix up slow sounds with quick sounds. Contrast high and low movements. Make up partner dances which are 'conversations' in movement and sound.
   I clap high and low
   You jump and slap your feet and turn
   with clicking fingers.
(See Messages **228.**)

121 CHANTS

Many of the lessons use chants as accompaniment. A chant is made by repeating and rhythmicizing a word or phrase. Word rhythms can come from almost any source. A few of the possibilities include:

people's names
street names
railway stations
advertisements
vegetables or flowers
numbers
food
games.

Repeat the words or word over and over again until a pattern emerges with clear accents and pauses. This rhythm can then be related to any appropriate action. Rhythms with a strong underlying beat tend to be translated into the feet or clapping movements. Non-metric rhythms (c a u l i f l o w e r) suggest body movements, such as opening and closing.

The following lessons use chants:

Red Indians **205**
Feet **225**
Stamping elephant
Humbug **233**
Rain dance **234**
Sausages and chips **231**
Names **229**
Hickory Dickory Dock **226**

122 ADVERTISEMENTS

Make a collection of advertisements from magazines or newspapers. The movement might be related to the meaning as well as the rhythm of the words. For example, 'Equal rights for wide feet!' (a shoe advertisement) — make rhythms of small steps and large steps feet in the air, feet on the ground or *'Let the train take the strain'* — a travelling step in a file, increasing the size and pace of the movement.

123 SONGS

Many songs can be used for their mood or meaning. Collections of folk songs on record, such as *World of Folk* (SPA 132), contain a variety of rhythms and moods. The rhythm and phrasing of a song can be used as accompaniment for action. Sometimes the words and meanings can be used too. (See **169** 'A Canny Lad the Miner', for help in using songs.)

Small movements of the shoulders, hands or feet can often be combined with classroom songs such as in the BBC *Music Time* programme.

The following BBC cassettes are very useful: *Bang on a Drum* MRMC 004) *Pete Seeger, Abiyoyo and other Story Songs for Children* (XTRA).

As with any other stimulus the method is to: select movement content ideas, and develop these in rhythmic phrases, using the song as a framework. (See also **168** Work songs, **109** Harvest, **105** Carols.)

124 'OH I DO LIKE TO BE BESIDE THE SEASIDE'

This song stimulated a seaside scene. The selected movement ideas were: clear *sequences* of travelling steps (galloping, hopping, skipping combinations) and *body shapes* connected to seaside actions.

The children each worked with a partner to produce a unison travelling action. They then joined two other children and decided upon *seaside activities,* such as

swimming movements

throwing and catching a ball

wave movements

shaking water off themselves

digging in the sand.

The teacher helped to make the movement dance-like by developing simple rhythmic phrases of movement, for example:

wave: rise and sink, RISE and sink, R I S E and sink.

digging: dig and throw, dig and throw, dig and THROW.

In groups of four the children made 'seaside pictures' by moving and stopping. The stopping was like a photograph of someone digging or swimming.

The dance evolved as a partner dance, groups of four, a file to end.

The partners danced to meet each other. They worked in groups of four to produce a sequence of seaside pictures. Finally they danced off the beach in follow-my-leader files. There was a great variety of movement and body shapes throughout.

125 ACTION SONGS AND RHYMES

If chants are chosen which give opportunity for plenty of qualitative action, rather than copying the appearance of something or someone, then the movement experience can be of value.

It is also important to select chants which give sufficient time for the full enactment of the action(s) or phrase. There is little scope for improvement in a rapid succession of images. It is often possible to elongate a part of the chant through repeating a line or only using one part of the chant over and over again. As with the poems, the rhythm rather than the words can accompany the movement and in this case it is easier to develop one kind of movement more creatively.

126 'THIS LITTLE PUFFIN'

Elizabeth Matteson's book contains many useful examples. The chant may be developed in a dance or be used to encourage a particular movement experience in the starting activities. Chants can be used as a basis for directed or creative activities.

> Jump-jump! Kangaroo Brown,
> Jump-jump! Off to town;
> Jump-jump! Up hill and down,
> Jump-jump! Kangaroo Brown.

Use it for jumping practice.

Jump all the way through the verse rather than following the words. Try jumps with the feet together or apart and together. Or:

> Jumps that take you forward.
> Jumps that turn you round.

> The wheels on the bus go round and round,
> Round and round, round and round.
> The wheels on the bus go round and round,
> All day long.

Select this *one* verse for whole body movement:

> Stretch up on the toes.
> Draw huge wheels in front of the body, stretching
> upwards, sideways and downwards as you do so
> One group at a time could perform the movement while the others chant
> Other ways of going 'round and round' might be explored.

> We all clap hands together,
> We all clap hands together,
> We all clap hands together,
> As children like to do.
> We all stand up together ...
> We all sit down together ...
> We all stamp feet together...
> We all turn round together...

is a good song for a variety of actions. Stress can be place on improvement, such as really stretching the feet, really going high, using the arms with the legs.

Each verse could be repeated several times to allow the movement to 'get going'. Organize the children so that they dance a group at a time. Have them sitting in different parts of the hall.

Gallop one two three four
Jump one two three and four
Turn around swiftly
And sit upon the floor.
Clap one two three four
Nod one two three four
Jump up again
And be ready for more.

This rhyme is a useful basis for linking actions together. Ways of turning and sitting could form the creative part of the lesson. A little dance might be evolved, such as outlined below:
Half the class could accompany the dancers by chanting or clapping the verse three times.

127 NURSERY RYHMES

Nursery rhymes can be used in a similar fashion. Sometimes use the rhythm alone, sometimes the rhythm and meaning. Brian Wildsmith's *Mother Goose* offers a good collection of rhymes and illustrations.

The rhyme 'Hot Cross Buns' can be used for walking and running. At the end of each line point to a new direction.

Hot cross buns
Walk walk walk
Hot cross buns
Walk walk walk
One a pen-ny Two a pen-ny
Run run run run run run run run
Hot cross buns
Walk walk stop.

You can make a 'cross' shape with legs or arms or whole body as you jump to the rhythm.

It is obvious that by looking at the rhyme in various ways different possibilities occur. Again, any of the above could be taught as clear examples to the children or arise out of creative movement through questions.

Other useful nursery rhymes
    'Ding dong bell' for stretching and pulling
    'Ride a cock-horse' for gallop and stop
    'Hey diddle diddle' for a sequence of action
    'Cobbler, cobbler mend my shoe' for skip and skip and stamp
    stamp stamp.
(See 'Hickory, Dickory Dock **226**.)
The record *Playtime* (SH M818) is a useful collection of rhymes, songs and dances. Remember that the children can ignore the words and dance to the rhythm only.

Poetry

128 POEMS AND DANCE

Words are used throughout this book, both to stimulate and categorize movement. Poems are one of the best sources for vivid word ideas. Many of the other stimuli could be linked to a poem. Poetry and dance are very akin to each other. Encourage children to collect poems they enjoy. The teacher might use the poem as a source of movement ideas for herself or read the poem to the children as a stimulus for their creative movement. A list of useful poetry books is included at the end of this section.

129 INTRODUCING THE POEM

It is important to decide how the poem is to be introduced. Some poems are too long or complex to be introduced in the dance lesson and should be read and discussed beforehand. Other poems are best used immediately and spontaneously during the lesson. Sometimes basic movement work related to the poem is best worked on before the poem is introduced.

The teacher must assess the most suitable method. The aim is a clear dance response with every part of the body fully extended and participating. The teacher must evaluate what aspect of the poem will stimulate this response. The dance will usually reflect the mood and general aura of the poem, although not slavishly interpreting it.

130 POEM AND ACCOMPANIMENT

Words or phrases from the poem can be used as a rhythmic or qualitative accompaniment. The mood or images may suggest a particular type of voice sound or percussion accompaniment — smooth and quiet or loud and vigorous.

It is also possible to divide up a longer poem in the following way:
a part of it is spoken
a part is selected for development into dance
and a part initiates a short percussion or sound piece.
These are but a few of the many possibilities of linking words, sounds and movement in very simple ways.

131 SELECTING MOVEMENT CONTENT

As with any other stimuli, selection of a *few* ideas and a limited movement framework for those ideas is essential. Do not try to perform an enactment of a whole poem, but select words or phrases as starting points to action. Some words will stimulate actual actions (jump twist). Some will suggest *how* to move (slowly suddenly). Others will suggest a mood or atmosphere. Others can be used as a rhythm. Never use a poem for movement until the children are warmed up mentally and physically, responsive to listening and moving. Avoid lengthy discussions. Listen, select, move.

132 'CAT'

'Cat' by Eleanor Farjeon in *That Way and This, Poetry for Creative Dance* (Chatto & Windus) contains some very expressive ideas:

> Cat!
> Scat!
> Atter her, atter her,
> Sleeky flatterer,
> Spitfire chatterer,
> Scatter her, scatter her
> Off her mat!
> Wuff!
> Wuff!
> Treat her rough!
> Git her, git her,
> Whiskery spitter!
> Catch her, catch her,
> Green-eyed scratcher!
> Slathery
> Slithery
> Hisser,
> Don't miss her!
> Run till you're dithery,
> Hithery
> Thithery
> Pfitts! pfitts!
> How she spits!
> Spitch! Spatch!
> Can't she scratch!
> Scritching the bark
> Of the sycamore-treé
> She's reached her ark
> And's hissing at me
> Pfitts! pfitts!
> Wuff! wuff!

                    Scat,
                    Cat!
                    That's
                    That!

Here the qualitative words suggest how to move and can be used for
sound accompaniment too, such as:

        P f i t t s ! P f i t t s !

or

        S l a t h e r y
        S l i t h e r y
        H i s s e r .

Use 'Pfitts!' as an accompaniment for strong sudden movements:

Pfitts! leaping from a crouch position into a wide stretched shape
Pfitts! shooting the fingers (like cat claws) high or across the body
        or behind
Pfitts! rolling and then shooting the legs high, arms outstretched.
        Balance there like a cat at bay.

Make sure the children experience fully at least one of the above.
Then encourage them to make a phrase of two or three 'pfitts' movements.

The 'Slithery' phrase could be a *smooth*, twisting, turning *movement* performed in unison by the class or group.

The sounds could be tape recorded and used as accompaniment, or
the children could accompany themselves as they move.

Other sound/action phrases in the poem might be similarly used.

133 'ON THE NING NANG NONG'

   by Spike Miligan in *Rhyme and Rhythm — Blue Book*
   (Gibson & Wilson)

On the Ning Nang Nong
Where the Cows go Bong!
And the Monkeys all say Boo!
There's a Nong Nang Ning
Where the trees go Ping!
And the tea-pots Jibber Jabber Joo.
On the Nong Ning Nang
All the mice go Clang!
And you just can't catch 'em when they do!
So it's Ning Nang Nong!
Cows go Bong!

Nong Ning Nang!
Trees go Ping!
Nong Ning Nang!
The mice go Clang!
What a noisy place to belong,
Is the Ning Nang Ning Nang Nong.

This is another poem where the words can be used as accompaniment. 'Ning, Nang, Nong' is obviously a mad place. Use the words 'clang', 'bong' and 'ping'. Relate the words to action.

The children could say and move the words in a number of strange ways.

Perhaps: 'Ning, Nang, Nong', strange walks, strange jumps, or strange arm gestures.

Again one line might be chosen for a unison class action.

Other Spike Milligan poems are to be found in *Round about Six*, by Margaret Rawlins.

134 'WIND', 'SNOWFLAKES' AND 'SNAKE'

Words used for their sounds as well as their meaning may be selected from many poems. Children enjoy using the action words to accompany the movement. The words give rhythm and quality.

In the poem 'Wind in the Trees' from *There's Motion Everywhere* by John Travers Moore

'Sweep — swaying,
Sweep — swaying,

beautifully conveys the undulating movement of trees in the wind.

The poem 'Snowflakes' appears in the same book. The word 'swirling' (among others) might be selected as an action and accompaniment. Beautiful illustrations accompany the poem too, and heighten the movement stimulus.

In 'The Snake' (another poem in his book) the words

'This way
That way
Back again'

could accompany the twisting, turning movement depicted in the illustration.

135 'WHISKY FRISKY' AND 'DRY BONES'

The rhythm of a poem may be selected for dancing. In 'Whisky Frisky', a poem about a squirrel in *Junior Voices*, edited by Geoffrey Summerfield (Penguin Educational) the rhythm of the words

'Whisky Frisky,
Hipperty hop'
can be:
clapped
stamped
jumped
or hopped
to a clapped, spoken or percussion accompaniment, Different
combinations of groups, sounding and moving, can be tried.
In the same way the poem 'Dry Bones' in *That Way and This* has a
refrain:
'Dem bones dem bones gonna walk around
Dem bones dem bones gonna walk around
Dem bones dem bones gonna walk around
Now hear the word of the Lord.'
This can be chanted and clapped by one group, while another
group moves: (a) with joint-jerking walks; (b) trying to use every part
of the body with the rhythm.

136 'STOCKING AND SHIRT'

The poem 'Stocking and Shirt' by James Reeves in *A Puffin Quartet
of Poets* and *That Way and This* has many times provided a clear
action framework for phrases of dance.
(a) clothes dancing on the line fastened on by a hand, a toe etc.
opening, closing, swinging.
(b) big downward tugging movements (the clothes in the wind)
(c) skipping and turning high (the clothes blow away)
(d) landing in 'screwed-up' shapes.
Body shapes and movements of different parts of the body can be
clarified in this dance.
Accompaniment Tambourine-shaking and beating. (See also
232-235.)

137 FIVE POEMS BY CHILDREN

Expression in dance and language seem to go together. The vividness
and vitality of the dance experience often spontaneously spill over
into language. With young children this may be through talking
with the teacher, or recapturing some of the words and rhythms used
in the dance lesson. Older children, stirred by the 'whole body' dance
movements and rhythms, will write their own poems. From a dance
experience, these poems always have a freshness and vitality and can

themselves be used for future classes. Often the poems are illustrated. The following poems arose from a dance class using action words and rhythms (as in 181). In a later lesson particular words and phrases were selected and practised as movement examples. Each pair of children then produced a short dance based on the selection of a word or phrase. The variety of movements and relationships was very wide.

Moving

Round, round, round I go
Quick, quick, quick I go
Moving slowly

Moving quick
Spinning like a spinning top
Jumping like a Frog
My finger moving
I hear a shout my body trembles
My body is moving all over now.

Lucy Wilson (ten years old)

Fast and Slow

Fast and slow fast slow
slow swift fast sweet
fast slow

Faster and faster the wind
blew blew on your face
slow slow slow moving

In and out in and out
moving swiftly through the trees.

Caroline Coles

Swinging

Look, look quickly look
I am swinging, I am swinging look I am swinging
look, look quickly look
I am leaping

Let's go down to the mill on the hill
look, look, I am grinding the mill
quick, quick, let's leave the mill and
go to the top of the hill.

Christopher Jackson

Movement

Flip, flop, flip
Moving the lip
The toe goes deep
And the hand goes dip

Lip, lip, lip
Doing your skip
Do the turn
And shake your hands

Skip, skip, skip
Doing your kick
Do the jump
And move your hip.

Jayen Patel

A class poem (to encourage a quick flow of ideas), produced by nine-year-old children immediately after a dance lesson, built up from movement words and their associations.

Leap horse
tumble kick roll
skip jump
fall hurt
stick stuck table
slide snake
rushing wind
rain drop
run boy
tumble
fall fall flop
creep crashes
car motor bike chopper
tree crashes
lightning thunder
lightning makes a pattern in the sky
trembling shaking
quivering wobbling
a flower growing
rain on the window.

Stories

138 STORY TO MOVEMENT

Existing stories can be good sources of movement ideas if it is remembered that rhythm and action movement quality and relationships rather than mime are the basic materials of dance. Many of the stimuli in this book could be related to a specific story or situation if the teacher so wished. For example, 'The Tunnel' lesson might be used with the Greek myth, 'The Minotaur in the Labyrinth', or red crêpe-paper streamers used to symbolize fire in a 'Fire of London' dance. The exploration in dance terms would remain the same.

Look around in the classroom and choose stories suitable for dance. Remember to:
    sectionize
    pick out or provide action words
    provide rhythmic accompaniment
    consider the dance form.
The following story illustrates the selecting of movement ideas from a mass of detail.

139 AN ENORMOUS DRAGON

He lives alone in the forest. He is dark green in colour and eats berries and leaves. Sometimes he travels down to the nearby village. All the people are very frightened and run away and hide until he leaves. Really he is a very friendly dragon and only wants some company. He sits down in the square and cries. The people approach him carefully and gradually realize that he will not harm them. They also discover that he is a very warm creature who is nice to snuggle up to, and will always blow some warmth into their houses. Soon he is living happily in the village with all the people.

This is a shortened version of a story made up by a group of children. The story could be acted out as a mime. To bring about a dance experience, certain action words must be selected as a basis for movement invention:
    the dragon — slithers, leaps, lashes
    the people — listen, run, hide.
Each of these actions must be phrased and made dance-like using perhaps level direction and body shape in the development.

Half the class might perform dragon-type movements, while the other half performs as the people.

Accompaniment

One class used the word 'Enormous' as accompaniment for their large movements. Use a cymbal for the dragon and tambour beats for the people.

140 MAKING UP A STORY FROM MOVEMENT WORDS

Here, the method is to select and develop suitable contrasting movements and then add imagery to the movement. The imagery should make the movement more vivid, not detract from it.

For example, first explore the movements: rush, struggle, crawl, balance.

Then ask, 'Where might we be when we make these movements?' Imagery of forests, quicksands or a bombsite might arise. In using this approach for the first time, the teacher might have to provide the imagery herself, but children are usually quick to offer ideas which the movement has suggested to them.

This method gives more scope for creativity in imagery and movement than using an existing story, but either may provide a valid starting point.

141 A DREAM—A FANTASY OF BODY PARTS

This can evolve by experimenting with strange movement of different body parts. Quick or slow movements can be explored.

For example, in the dream our legs are very, very long. We stride with enormous steps. Our arms start twisting and turning like snakes, up and down. They get knotted together. We pull them apart. Our legs turn to rubber. We bounce about into strange shapes. Our heads begin to shake, then our whole body. We stop suddenly. Then begin to grow bigger and bigger until we burst.

All the movement can of course be defined clearly in phrases. This story encourages awareness of body parts, and many other variations are possible. This example might be a culmination of the children's ideas or be used as an initial example to stimulate their creativity (see Body parts 16).

142 MAGIC STORIES

Many stories for infants and juniors are about magical happenings. The teacher should select extracts from the story rather than trying to express the whole story in movement. The story might be one created by the children or an existing tale such as 'Aladdin' or '*My Friend Mr Leakey*' by J.B.S.Haldane. (Mr Leakey is a magician who travels the world on a magic carpet and encounters strange situations and characters en route.)

Remember that the lesson needs action variety so select contrasting movement ideas. The children can work initially on their own. The teacher may accompany with percussion or suitable extracts from 'atmospheric music'.

Use movement phrases arising from:

The magic-carpet ride (in place) — rise and sink with gentle floating movements up and down. Balance on different body parts. Roll off as the carpet lands in the:

Land of serpents — use writhing and wriggling, rising and sinking, travelling along the ground fast on the stomach, back or side.

Ride off on the carpet again and land in: the land of giants. Use huge, stamping strides, large, jumping turns, huge arm gestures.

Ride off on the carpet and land . . . etc.

Use any ideas which will give movement contrasts, such as magic-horse land, volcano land, no gravity, whirlpool.

Infant children could alternate between moving near and with the teacher for the magic-carpet ride and moving on their own in their own space for the different lands, Juniors enjoy creating sequences in groups. Each group depicts a 'land'. All the groups join together in a unison sequence for the magic-carpet ride.

143 MAGIC WORDS

When chanted and repeated as word rhythms, these are another movement source:

Salamandino!
>   say it
>   clap it
>   stamp it
>   jump it
>   travel it.

Each group can work on different magic words. One group may begin in a circle. The first child chants and moves to the magic word. The other children copy his movement and chant with him many times. Then the next child chants and does *his* movement to the magic word. All copy, so that each child in the group contributes a phrase of movement and the phrase is repeated and consolidated by everyone, for example:

First child — 'Salamandino! Salamandino!'

Jump and turn. Jump and turn (many times)

Rest of group — Repeat the above.

The dance could end with the children deciding what *happens* to them as a result of the magic words.

They explode or get stuck together (see Chants **121** and **236 - 8**).

Myths from other Countries

144 SOURCES

Use stories and music, festivals and customs from other countries as
dance sources. Simple action phrases, groupings and floor patterns
will arise. The *Larousse Encyclopedia of Mythology* is a rich store of
information, as the following example illustrates.

145 THE FOUR GODS (CHINA)

From the many exciting and colourful stories and descriptions the
following idea is selected as a framework for dance. Each year the
numerous gods and goddesses assembled before the greatest of the
gods, the August Personage of Jade. They would report on their
activities and he would either praise or rebuke them.

Method

Four gods are selected. Each can be characterized by a particular way
of moving.

The Moon Goddess begins in a curved body shape. She dances
lightly, tracing curves in the air with her fingertips on a curving floor
pattern.

The Thunder God alternates strong, thrusting arm movements
with stamping leaps and strongly-held positions.

The Whirlwind God whirls in place and makes huge circles on the
floor.

The Dragon God uses big whipping movements, sudden turns and
sudden stops.

Group formation

Each type might be characterized by a group of children. The group
formation could be considered:

Moon Goddess Group — From a starting position within the
group weave in and out on a *curving floor pattern* and return to the
beginning position.

Thunder God Group — a circle. Alternate children leap into the
centre and out again.

Suggested accompaniment — a different percussion sound for each
group, e.g. cymbals, triangles. The instrument could be played by a
member of the group or by the teacher. Alternatively, Chinese music
might be played quietly as a background for the movement.

146   HAND SHAPES WITH CHINESE MUSIC

The music could also be used to stimulate another dance based on hand shapes and patterns which are formed very lightly and delicately (like Chinese paintings). Holding the hands well in front of the body, touch together different parts of the hands and see what shapes you make:

little finger to thumb
back of the wrist to the front of the wrist
twist the wrists.

Make a dance based on a simple follow-my-leader travelling step to arrive in group shapes where the hands are important.

Masks and tunics
Masks and dragon-emblazoned tunics can be made. One class symbolized the August Personage by a huge picture of him, painted on cloth, and pinned on a wall as a focus for the whole idea.

147   OLAV AND THE MOUNTAIN TROLLS

This is a splendid tale of princesses stolen away from the palace garden by ugly trolls and finally rescued after much trial and tribulation by the hero, Olav.

It is important to remember that a story must be divided into sections and that a simple movement idea must then be chosen to represent each section. The above outline of the story is sufficient stimulus for movement. The inclusion of too many details (of what happened or what Olav did) means that the concentration is on story idea rather than movement. Choose limited starting points so that the movement can 'grow'.

The princesses
   creep and pause, creep and pause
   skip and turn
   run and crouch
   crawl and roll.
The trolls appear.
   They stride and freeze in fierce positions
   (stride, stride, stride, *freeze*)
   leap and freeze.
   push and push and freeze.

The rhythms, body shapes and levels can be practised and clarified over a number of lessons. *All* the phrases should be worked on by *all* the children before any groups are arranged. Choose perhaps two contrasting actions to work on in one lesson and do not attempt a dance form until the action is lively and inventive.

Beware of using an extended idea which might be beyond the children's span of interest. Young children might prefer to do a 'Troll dance' and experience the other movement material through different stimuli.

One class evolved a dance as follows:

The princesses began in a group shape then crept into the garden, from different positions and at different levels. They made a skipping dance with definite arm movements and steps, towards and away from a huge paper flower symbolizing the garden. Two files of trolls then surrounded the centre group of princesses, danced around them and then 'pushed' them with magic pushes out through a tunnel (formed by six children) into the 'bad regions'. They were not 'rescued' in the dance, which did not seem to bother them. Perhaps the rescue could be enacted in a song or a piece of creative music. This form would of course be valueless if it were just imposed on the children without prior movement exploration. The form evolves from the movement and collaboration with the children.

Again, simple costumes, crowns and stocking head-dresses decorated with green crêpe hair were made for the dance. Avoid any costume which hinders the movement.

The accompaniments
   woodblock for creeping
   recorded music from 'Voices' Book *Pastoral* for skipping
   a clear tambour beat rhythm for striding and leaping
   a gradual crescendo on a cymbal for the pushing and crawling.

148 MAUI AND THE SUN (NEW ZEALAND)

'How Maui made the sun slow down' (from *Maori Myths and Tribal Legends*) relates how the sun was thought to rise each morning from a deep pit. The days were short because the sun crossed the sky too quickly and so Maui and his brothers decided upon a plan that would slow the sun down and make the days longer. They travelled cautiously by night until they came to the pit where the sun lay. As he rose up they captured him, tied him with ropes, and beat him fiercely. The sun struggled fiercely, but gradually became weaker, and to this day has moved slowly on his course across the sky.

The movement possibilities are many:

(a) *The sun rising and sinking*
   rising and sinking movements
   opening and closing.

These phrases could be practised by individuals, partners or small groups using contrasting body parts leading the movement.

(b) *The shape of the sun*
   This might be symbolized by a means of a circle which moves towards the centre and away or around with appropriate rounded-arm gestures.

(c) *The hunters*
   crawl, slither and pause.
   Make variations through changes of speed and weight on different body parts.

(d) *The hunter and the sun* — a partner dance.
   One whips and holds
   one struggles and droops.

Select from these ideas and draw the ideas together to make a dance. Have half the class in the centre of the room (the sun group); half the class in a large circle at the edges of the room (the hunters).

Accompaniment

Have one sound for the sun rising strongly and one sound for the hunters creeping. Or use music such as *Traditional Maori Songs* as a background to the movement.

The dance

  (a) The sun and the hunters move alternately several times so that a rhythm of rising and sinking and freezing alternates with crawling, slithering and pausing. One group freezes when the other group moves. Everyone is still.

  (b) Moving a few at a time, the hunters each seize a partner from the central sun group. The teacher accompanied the actions of run, seize and pull to a space. The partners hold their positions until all are spaced out.

  (c) A partner dance using whipping and struggling. Encourage the children to 'move and be still', to watch each other so that the dance is built on action and reaction.

Work on the material over a number of lessons. Everyone would experience all the phrases before the groups were established, and again only *part* of the above might be selected for movement.

149 SUN FOLLOW-UP WORK

A large mural of the sun using and combining 'hot' colours in paint or coloured tissue-paper could be made.

The following poems, by a ten-year-old, resulted from discussion after the dance on feelings and thoughts about the sun.

The Sun

The sun came out
the moon went in
day and night goes by
the sun went in
the moon came out

The sun is hot
the moon is cold
hot cold sun moon
days go by nights
go by.

Caroline Coles

Pictures

150 ILLUSTRATIONS

A good illustration can reinforce a movement idea or provide the initial *stimulus*. Look at the picture and relate it to movement. It may suggest: the action of people or things; a particular quality of movement which can be developed.

151 SOURCES

Sources of pictures are, of course, many and varied. Many poetry books are illustrated and such illustrations are often good movement stimuli because, like poems, they abstract a particular idea and present it uncluttered by other details. Children's books, magazines and periodicals (such as *Child Education*), paintings and pictures around the school are other obvious sources for movement ideas. Take care to choose a picture which does have immediate movement associations.

Encourage children to make collections of pictures or photographs which show different movements or qualities.

152 FAIRGROUND PHOTOGRAPH

The photograph in *Wordscapes* by Barry Maybury shows children on a *roundabout*. This suggests rising and sinking. Partners take hands and find a stepping rhythm: down down up up, down down up up. Small groups might join hands in the centre and alternate moving smoothly up and down. Other action sequences are suggested by the movements of people or machines at a fair.

Use 'Fairground Music' from *Mechanical Organs* (AMB AFL 102); (see Swingboats 27).

153 LIGHTNING PHOTOGRAPH

Use an illustration which suggests:
   fast, shooting movements of the arms
   thrusting leaps
   sinking down gently; stillness.
Suggest that the children move in sudden phrases of action, and then be quite still. For accompaniment, use a soft beating on a cymbal with occasional loud accents as a background to the children's movement rhythms.

154 'GAMES' BY BRUEGHEL

This painting is a very good movement stimulus for action phrases. Remember that actions must be selected and given a clear rhythmic framework. Different relationships in pairs or small groups are also illustrated. Children may use the movements they see in the painting, but also add their own game movements (see Games 171-9).

Suggest playing with something on your own, for example with an imaginary ball or hoop then working with a partner.

One class of children made the following dance using:

(a) *Partner activities*
    hoop movement: arm circles and rolling
    leapfrog: a sequence of bend down, jump over,   bend down, both *fall* over
    hitting with a stick: hit, hit, hold still
    partner action and reaction: dodge, dodge, freeze.

(b) The whole class made a sudden stop with 'feet off ground' leading to

(c) Follow-my-leader files using interweaving floor patterns.

The music was from UM 1300, a selection of lively mediaeval chants and tunes.

155 TELEVISION

Television offers an enormous range of visual stimuli. Current programmes such as

all suggest ways of moving and can give a framework for improvisation. School broadcasts showing movement of nature or people might be recorded and later used as a movement stimulus.

156 'GANGSTER

A television programme such as 'Gangster' shows:
    running and stopping
    slow-motion falling
    hiding under outstretched hands.

Try running and stopping from a variety of positions. Have two groups working alternately, one holding a position while the other one moves. Use a woodblock accompaniment.

Slow-motion falling — stretching out the body, falling forwards, backwards or sideways into different body shapes.
Use a cymbal.

Hiding — behind the hands at different levels, kneeling, crouching or lying down.
Use a tambour.

Each of the above would be practised in rhythmic phreases:
Ready . . .
Hide and still
Change position . . .
Hide and still

Each group makes a dance using the above material. Suggest they begin and end in a *group shape*, positioned close together.

Use a fast-moving piece of music, for example from the record *BBC Fourth Dimension* to accompany the movement.

157 'PINK PANTHER'

This suggests partner work: Leading and following — creep carefully one behind the other. Stop when the leader stops. Sudden surprise changes of direction or leadership. Other ways of 'following' — crawling, leaping, sidestepping. Devise a 'surprise' ending (see **239, 240**).

Colourful Locations

158 CHOOSING A SCENE

Choose a setting or scene as a starting point for ideas. Avoid trying to depict all the actions within a large scene, but rather abstract some movement qualities or actions that will symbolize the scene. Remember the narrower the selection the greater the possibility of movement development. One advantage of using a place or colourful background is that other aspects of the child's work — creative writing, painting etc. — can be linked to it and the scene might be shown through different media and link with many of the other stimuli. Select simple actions, phrases and body shapes as starting points. For example a ranch scene could be chosen where:

the cowboy whirls and throws a lasso

leaps and falls (from a bucking horse).

Use music from *Rodeo* by Aaron Copland.

Suggestions for other scenes:

Jungle (**236**)

Desert

Factory

Beach (see Seaside song **124**)

Oil rig

Mars (**241**)

The city

Circus (**243**)

The following diagram represents movement possibilities from one idea.

159 UNDERWATER DANCE

Each phrase could be developed by thinking *where* the movement goes in the space.

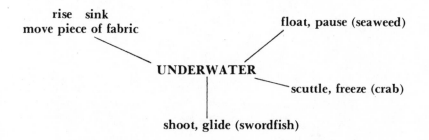

rise   sink
move piece of fabric

float, pause (seaweed)

UNDERWATER

scuttle, freeze (crab)

shoot, glide (swordfish)

160 WITCHES' DEN

A group of schools organized a Witch Afternoon. Classes from each school came together to make dance, sound effects and simple costumes. The hall was blacked out and decorated with witch paintings and strange mobiles. As he entered the Den each child was stamped with the Devil's Mark (a pig's trotter dipped in ink). The children danced in groups to voice chants and percussion (see **206**).

It is often a simple matter to enhance a dance with a few props which help to make the dance more vivid.

161 EXCURSIONS

Visits to museums, galleries and other places of interest may stimulate observations, drawing or writing which in turn could feed into dance. Recent examples have been of a visit to the North American Indian Exhibition (in London) and a visit to a steam museum.

Machines

162 MACHINE-LIKE MOVEMENT

Machines are often used as movement stimuli, but care must be taken to develop the movement.

The movement must involve and stretch the whole body. Begin with big movements. Stress the energy and power of machines. Small movements can grow later when the whole body involvement is present.

Visual stimuli are far more vivid then 'imagining' a machine. Look at machinery, such as:

a car engine
the inside of a watch
a home-made machine
a picture of a machine.

Ask what the parts of the machine *do*?

move up and down
round and round
vibrate.

These can then be related to a movement rhythm. Ask what do they *look like*?

long
round
bent
twisted

These shapes can be related to starting body shapes of individuals or groups.

163 AN ORANGE-CRUSHING MACHINE

The stimulus for this was a child's painting.

The *actions* selected were:

bending
stretching
circling
jerking

(a) arm movements

stretching and bending. Moving high and deep — 'piston movement'.

(b) leg movements
   bend stretch, bend stretch
   If tried from different *starting*
   position (knees, back etc.) this demands real skill.
(c) trunk and arm movements
   huge stretching *circles*
   jerking forwards, sideways, backwards.

The accompaniment was provided initially by clear word and tambour rhythms from the teacher; later, the children made voice sounds.

Dances were made in groups of three. Each group evolved an ending by choosing to:

accelerate

slow down or

get stuck

The above example is rich in movement content.

The above ideas evolved with a group of ten-year-olds. Younger children might work on whole body movements to produce simple 'up-and-down' machines; 'round-and-round' machines.

164 MACHINES IN STORIES

Children's stories very often contain exciting machine imagery. It is often enough to relate the lesson loosely to the story to spark off interest in the movement. Good examples are the machines in *Charlie and the Chocolate Factory* by Roald Dahl and *The Flying Machine* by Oliver Postgate and Peter Firmin.

165 A CLASS MACHINE

An exciting end to a lesson which explores different kinds of machine-like movements is to have the whole class become one enormous machine.

Method

The children sit around the edge of the room. One child begins in the centre of the room and establishes a clear phrase of machine-like movement. The next child comes beside him and 'fits in' with a similar or contrasting movement. Then the next child and the next child and so on until the whole class has joined the central group and made the machine.

Suggest the children all use a different body part and different directions.

Try the idea again, adding voice sounds: one child moves strongly up and down with cha *bom*, cha *bom* . . . and the one next to him uses arms moving out and in with sst *da da*, sst *da da* . . .

Accompaniment
Make repetitive voice sounds or use percussion accompaniment or music with a clear beat such as 'reggae' from *Your Body Working and Dancing* (XX1209).

Poems about machinery can be found in *That Way and This — Poetry for Creative Dance* (see **244**).

Work Dances

166 OCCUPATIONAL ACTIONS

Traditional work dances are to be found throughout the world. Children can make their own work dances by observing the occupational actions that go on around them.

heaving
washing
cleaning
lifting
digging
chopping
pulling
typing

These can spring from locations such as a:

fishing boat
office
coal mine
factory
launderette
oil rig
house
building site

(See also **158**.)

167 WORK RHYTHMS AND WASHDAY

Choose a phrase of simple repetitive action, and provide a voice rhythm to go with the action, such as pull and pull and PULL (on a rope).

Repeat it many times. Enlarge the action so that the whole body is participating. Make the arms stretch far from the body ready for the pull.

Any sequence of movements can be made rhythmic through repetition such as washing clothes.

Use the actions of:
rubbing the clothes
lifting them up and
dunking them down.

Use the rhythm
Rub - rub rub - rub and LIFT and *press* down and
Rub - rub rub - rub and LIFT and *press* down.

The rubbing involves movement of the whole arm. The lifting and pressing down uses stretching high and bending low. Partners might use the same movements and rhythm but at different times, i.e. a dance 'round'. Other phrases might be added, such as:

 shake them out and *peg* them or
 lift the clothes and *place* them.

Accompaniment
Use words, percussion or music such as the song 'Sweepy, Sweepy, Sweepy' (this includes Washy, Washy!) from *Abiyoyo and Other Story Songs for Children by Pete Seeger* (on cassette ZCXTR 1066 XTRA) or 'Watersplash music', from *John Peel's Archive Things* (REC 68 M).

168 WORK SONGS

Many folk-song collections contain work songs. The rhythm of the music and the meaning of the words can be used for dance. It is important to repeat selected phrases of action rather than attempting to interpret literally *all* the actions in the song.

169 'A CANNY LAD THE MINER'

This song, by Ian Campbell from *The World of Folk* (SPA A132) gives a marvellously vivid description of the miner's hard life. He's 'up in the morning and out in the frost'. Then down to the 'dark and heat' of the mine, 'sweating and strainin' and strivin' for air'.

Try building a group dance to show the hard work of the miner. Select three working actions from the song:

 hewing
 filling
 pushing

as a basis for action phrases. Each group might use all three words and develop them into a sequence of action. Develop an awareness of where the action takes place and the relationship of each child to another, using contrasts of level.

Or, more simply, each group uses one word which can be performed at a medium or fast pace.

All the above ideas are worked out using the rhythm of the song as an accompaniment. Everyone practises ideas with the teacher and then each group evolves its own simple dance.

The dance form

As the song stresses the 'endless round' of the miner's life, the dance might be enacted in a circle formation. Each group performs in place and then travels round to the next place.

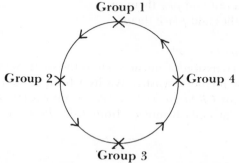

To end the dance the miners could step into the centre of the circle, and gradually raise their arms higher and higher to 'breathe fresh air again' as the 'cage' ascends. There is a 'Net Hauling Song', also on *The World of Folk* which could be reated similarly.

The record *Your Body Working and Dancing* (XXI 209) contains more music for work dances.

170 SEA SHANTIES

'Boney was a Warrior' and 'What shall we do with a Drunken Sailor?' are both examples of 'hauling' shanties (hauling up the sails). A whole dance can be built on 'hauling' variations. Try humming the song. Without the words it is often easier to fit movements to the rhythm. Develop the quality of the movement and partner relationships:

   haul together or
   one after the other
   with changes of position.

Capstan Shanties such as the 'Rio Grande' can be used for pushing actions in a circle formation. Vary by pushing with the hands, the side or the back.

Accompaniment

Have half the class singing, half moving, or use recorded music, such as 'The Shanty Set' on the record *Ring of Iron* (TSR 016) or 'Sea Songs and Shanties'.

There is a full description of sea shanties in *Grove's Dictionary of Music and Musicians*.

Games

171 CHOOSING GAMES

Find out what games the children play and assess whether they could be used as movement frameworks. Refer to *The Lore and Language of Schoolchildren* by Iona and Peter Opie (Oxford University Press). Choose games which give scope for variations. Many games involve complex patterns of skipping, jumping and hopping which can be linked to the dance work. Game ideas may grow into complete dances by developing variations, beginnings and endings.

172 'FEET OFF GROUND'

Run and stop when the drum stops beating, with feet off the ground.
  To vary, try lifting the feet and legs in different ways:
  feet high in a shoulder stand
  balanced in a sitting position, arms and legs off the ground
  lying on the stomach, 'flying' — lifting arms and legs.
The above game might be posed as a creative challenge or one or two examples taught and improved to strengthen the body and provide examples for future exploration. Alternatively the children might choose what parts of their bodies are *on* the ground, for example, two feet and one hand on the ground, with the rest of the body stretching out. This idea is further exemplified in Musical Bumps.

173 MUSICAL BUMPS

Children seem quite happy with game distortions. They serve to rouse the movement imagination. Six-year-olds enjoyed a 'sort of musical bumps', which involved bouncing down onto the floor on different body parts. Musical Bumps that went wrong, perhaps?

174 'HE' OR TAG

Organize the children into four groups. Two groups move at a time. Each group occupies half the hall space. Each group plays 'he'. When the tambour is playing they run and dodge. When it stops they freeze. Music can also be used, such as 'The Chase' *BBC Radiophonic* (REC 25M). Turn down the volume or pause for the 'freeze' movement (see **245**).

Improving the movement

Encourage the children to make the movement very vigorous, to dodge, duck, retreat and stop. Praise skilful changes of direction. Each child must imagine that he is being chased even when he is not, so that the whole room is full of dodging, ducking, swerving children.

Practise standing in place and dodging parts of the body. dodging hands—up, down, behind, as if that part of the body is avoiding being touched. Do this with short, sharp rhythms.

Two groups moving alternately

The two groups perform the 'He' dance alternately in their half of the hall. The teacher indicates which group is to move and which to stop, by saying: 'Ready, first group: dodge dodge dodge and *stop* (many times). Second group: dodge dodge dodge and stop etc.'

The idea may grow into a dance by developing an ending. For example when you are touched, you stand still, fall over, explode or stick together. Gradually everyone is standing still. There are many other possibilities.

175 IMAGINARY BALLS, ROPES, HOPSCOTCH ETC.

Throw an imaginary ball from one to the other. This is a good exercise for developing response to others.

Practice 'Prepare, throw and hold the release position'. Vary the way of throwing.

Imaginary use of:
balls
skipping ropes
hoops
hopscotch
swings
rocking horses
provokes keen movement

Method

The teacher calls out the activity:
'bouncing a ball'
'bowling a hoop'
'skipping with a skipping rope'.

The children must respond quickly, with a change of activity and rhythm. Make sure that the movement is really well performed, extending the whole body. Work for coordination and flow.

Develop one of the activities by finding variations (see **186** and **201** for more ideas).

176 HOPSCOTCH DANCE

Jump your feet apart and together
  apart and together.
Turn on the fourth jump.
Jump and balance on one leg with the other up behind you.
Copy your partner's movement.
Use 'Hopscotch', music by William Walton on the record *Listen, Move and Dance* (No. CLP 3162).

177 GRANDMOTHER'S FOOTSTEPS

This can be a basis for travelling in a variety of ways. Some of the ways can then be selected and arranged in sequences in follow-my-leader file dances. The initial limitation must be sufficient to provoke worthwhile movement, such as walking in large strides on all fours, with straight arms and legs, hopping with one leg high behind or jumping with the knees high in front.

178 BOX GAME

This game involve the use of:
  feet and legs
  hands and arms
  body
  head
Method
Paint a box. It becomes a movement dice. Print one of the above parts on each side of the box. With young children draw the body part.

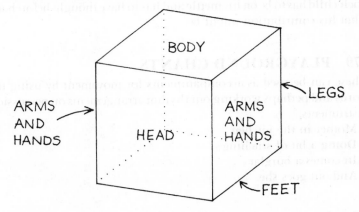

The children sit in a circle with one child holding the box in the centre.

The children clap one, two, three, four, five times.

The child in the centre throws the box in the air.

Whichever word on the box lands uppermost, the child must immediately improvise a repeated phrase of rhythmic movement using that part of the body.

For example, 'Hands and arms' lands uppermost, so swing the arms forwards and backwards and clap swing forwards . . .

Everyone copies and joins in, keeping the rhythm going, making a swing, clap dance. The teacher reinforces the rhythm. Music can be used for this if necessary. Fade the music (or the tambour) for the sign to the children to sit.

The child goes and sits behind another child, who then goes into the centre. He picks up the box, everyone claps five times. He throws. He decides on a movement etc.

The first time this game is tried, the teacher throws up the box, the children improvise. The teacher stimulates and improves the response. Suggest changes of level and speed to make the response different each time. The aim is variety, invention. Adapt the game to suit the children. One particular movement might be used for each body part.

This game has been used with great success by both primary and secondary children. The teacher needs of course to feed in the ideas initially. If done well, an atmosphere of absorprtion is produced through:

the clapping
the wait
the immediate action
the joining in and establishing of a movement
motif.

Each child has to be on his mettle and has to have thought beforehand what his contribution might be.

179 PLAYGROUND CHANTS

These can be used as accompaniments for movement by using the words and perhaps working out rhythm arrangements on percussion instruments.

Mother in the kitchen
Doing a bit of stitching
In comes a burglar
And out goes she.

Half the children clap or play. Half move. The children can work on skilful skipping steps which they relate to a partner, and then teach to another couple.

'Salt, mustard, vinegar, pepper' could be hopped, jumped, turned etc. and sequences of foot actions evolved.

Part 3

Remember to use
STARTING
ACTIVITIES
ACCOMPANIMENT
REPETITION

180   THE EXAMPLE LESSONS (GENERAL)

The example lessons indicate:

(a)   a selection of movement ideas from a stimulus.

(b)   the development of that material through examples, questions and tasks.

(c)   the sort of dance that might develop.

The *starting activities* which are an essential part of each lesson are listed under **24-32**.

The example lessons are intended to demonstrate *growth* of ideas and are not meant to be absolutely definitive. Alternative actions or images may also be relevant (see **57**). Some suggestions are made for *accompaniment.*

A great variety of language is used to keep the vitality and freshness of the movement, and avoid a sterotyped response. 'Asking in different ways' and 'Responding in different ways' are stressed.

The lessons give opportunity for *repetition* and growth of movement ideas in many contrasting contexts. Movement ability and awareness develop gradually over a period of time. The teacher must keep a balance between repetition and variety so that ideas are constantly reinforced and revitalized.

When working with young children the stress is on breadth of movement experience. Older children can remember movement in more detail. They can cope with more development *within* a phrase of movement, and enjoy creating and repeating dances.

Obviously there is much cross-sectioning possible between stimuli (see Index). A few lessons are more suitable for older children, some for younger, but a large percentage of them can be used for any age group, by adapting the language and development ideas.

It is hoped that the teacher will *select* relevant dance ideas and tasks for her class, and also use the lessons as a guide towards planning her own dances with children. In each lesson:

Remember to use
STARTING
ACTIVITIES
ACCOMPANIMENT
REPETITION

Imagery and Action Words

181 Action Dance

stretch
leap
roll run
fall

These words contrast in place and travel. They stress whole body involvement. They can be practised individually or in sequences. The following experiences help to build vocabulary and develop the joy of moving rhythmically. Task 8 'running' is particularly involving.

Accompaniment tambour and music such as BBC Radiophonic *Radio Nottingham*

Follow up
A group action painting from the ideas of running, falling, and rolling paint. Cover the paper with designs. Or make a movement poem.

Questions and Tasks

1 Stretch one hand up, up to the ceiling, then sideways so your whole body stretches sideways, and then drops down. Bend your knees. And again repeat the stretch on the other side,
   Stretch and stretch and down
   Stretch and stretch and down,
   as if you were trapped, reaching for the ceiling.

2 Now stretching upwards quickly, shoot your fingers upwards. . . Take it into jumping shooting upwards, really stretched, like trying to burst balloons above your head.

3 Now look around you for the spaces. Everyone leaping into a new space. Ready, really high:
   Leap, leap, leap, leap and balance.
4 Everyone copy that one. He's leaping from two feet back onto two, opening wide in the air (like a frog or Batman). All together:
   Leap and leap and leap and hold the position.
5 Listen. I am going to play six beats on the tambour. Take all the six beats to lie down on your backs slowly. Think how you go down . . . Relax.
6 Curl up tight on your side Now,
   Roll and stop and
   Roll back again.
   Once more. Ready . . .
7 Now roll and stretch up to standing. Who can do it smoothly? Good, I saw one of you then stretch your legs, then your arms, then your whole self upwards.
8 Listen to the tambour. As I point to you, run quickly and lightly in and out amongst the other children and back to your place. Don't touch anyone. See how fast and lightly you can run. (Point to about six children in quick succession, so six are running simultaneously.)
9 Now one person is going to run amongst you and past you. As he passes you, *fall* slowly to the ground and lie quite still. Ready . . . How are you falling?
10 All watch this one, Show them your turning fall.
11 Lie down. Listen to the music. Think of the movements we have used. Use these, and any others that occur to you, with the music. Make your dance. Show me when it stops.

The Dance

An individual dance
This may be very short, allowing a free choice of movement at the end of the lesson. This type of lesson, which gives scope for energetic, large movement, is taken at a fast pace with very clear directives throughout. Older, inexperienced children find security in working in this way. Do not try to develop the 'dance' too much at this stage. Listen to the music more thoroughly another lesson.

Summary

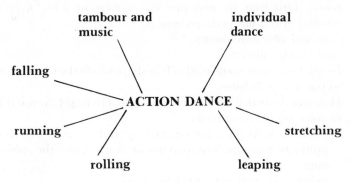

tambour and music   individual dance

falling

ACTION DANCE

running   stretching

rolling   leaping

182 FLYING

skipping
turning
dipping

The word 'flying' is used in an abstract sense to unify airborne movements. It could equally well be linked with ideas about birds. Note how definite sequences are given to develop the high, elevated quality. Once the children are absorbed *rhythmically*, variations will grow quite naturally.

Accompaniment music, e.g. 'German Dances' by Mozart.

Questions and Tasks
1   Listen to the music. Move on the spot with large skipping steps.
    Step hop and step hop.
  Lift the legs; make the movement large, rhythmic.
2   Now move round the room. All go the same way this time to avoid bumping.
    Step hop and step hop and into the air and step hop.

3   Good. Now let's see a group at a time so that you have plenty of room. This time try and vary the movement a bit. Keep the *rhythm* going but perhaps *turn* it:
   or add arm movements
   or change direction.
   Good, there were some really clear shapes with the legs stretched to the side or behind.
4   How can we link these ideas to the idea of flying? Can you think of some more flying ideas?
   Turning with the arms dipping up and down? Using flying jumps in a group, interweaving or moving into the centre or out?
   Side-to-side rocking with wide arms?
5   Make groups of four people. Decide how you are going to begin, facing or back to back or . . .
6   Listen to the music. When it pauses, stop quite still. Notice where you are in relationship to other people.

The Dance
Small group dances
From a simple beginning many group variations will develop through working in: files or circles, intermingling, following or contrasting.

Observe the response and help to clarify it. Alternatively feed in more ideas and tasks as in no. 4.

Summary

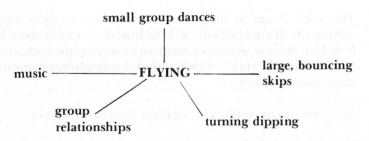

183   FREE FALL

falling

Stress body shape, and actions that *precede* and *follow* falling. Work with a partner. Use any imagery that arises, like 'falling through space'.

Accompaniment atmospheric Sound Effects (BBC REC 225) or BBC Radiophonic

Questions and Tasks

1   With the music try *collapsing* down very slowly. Start in a high, stretched position. Let the knees go, the elbows, the head, like melting.
2   Lie still for a moment. Feel really collapsed, heavy. Then *rise up slowly* into another stretch. *Balance* on any part of your body so you are all in different shapes.
    And slowly collapse again.
3   Try now *spiralling* down. Open the arms so that you look wide. You could travel across the floor.
4   With a *partner* now. Spiralling down one after another.
5   What do you do when you are down to the ground?
    Roll and come up again?
    Leap up?
6   What do you do before the fall?
    Run and fall. Everyone try that many times, or Leap and fall.
7   How could we make a dance called 'Free Fall'?

The Dance
A partner dance
The children dance, sometimes at the same time, sometimes one after the other. They use the image of people or stars 'falling through space'. The dance might end with 'suspended' shapes or collapse (disintegration) of everyone.

Summary

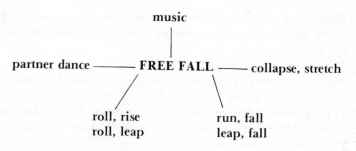

whirl
float
fall

These movements might be selected after an initial discussion about 'nightmares'. Use changes of *speed* and *sudden* stops. Stress *large* movements. Lie down or 'hang down' between each idea.

Accompaniment qualitative percussion or extract from 'Maxwell Davies' 'Turris Camparum Sonantium', or John Cage's 'Strange Amores', Voices Record 2.

Questions and Tasks

1   Begin by lying down. Listen to the music and *stand slowly* as if somebody is pulling you upwards. And stop. Hold your position.
2   Now begin whirling. You can't stop. You're caught up in whirling. And stop. Sink down slowly.
3   The whirling goes on but you can't turn round all the time. Try:
       arms whirling in front of the
       head circling running fast in a small circle
    or a mixture of these.
4   Now begin to build whirling movements with your partner. Fit in, be higher or lower. Sometimes move *fast*, sometimes *slow* down.
5   Yes, you could whirl each other.
6   Now *float* gently up and down, to another space, like treading on feathers. And stop.
7   Follow your *partner, floating* to another space. Make the movements very big. Float the arm high, the knee high. How do you fit in with your partner?
8   Show me some nightmare *falls*. What would they be like?

9 Good.
>   *Jerking* falls
>   *Spinning* down fast into a heap
>   Slowly *crumpling* etc.
Practise some of those with your partner.

The Dance
A partner dance

This may contain contrasts of speed. Make the beginning and ending position clear. Make it clear whether the partner's movement is the same or contrasting. The teacher might help the children form a common plan, such as:
whirling
slow-motion falling
disappearing
or the children could each decide on their own action order. They might choose *one* action only.

Follow up nightmare poems

Summary

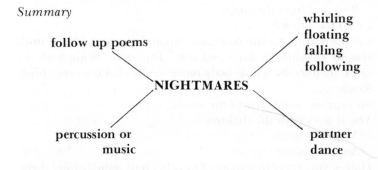

follow up poems

whirling
floating
falling
following

NIGHTMARES

percussion or
music

partner
dance

185   A PROCESSION

shaking
clapping
stepping

This lesson works first of all on *extending* and freeing the body, using pure action not related to an idea. Then the movement is arranged in a circle and the image of a gay procession used as a culmination to the lesson, The idea could be developed further in subsequent lessons.

Accompaniment steel-band music.

Questions and Tasks

1 (Everyone kneeling.) Imagine you are a piece of elastic and I am going to pull you out, stretch you into a shape. Ready, I pull your arms . . . your toe and arm so you have to balance on a hand and knee, really stretch (etc.)

2 Here's a phrase on the tambour . . . I want you to start kneeling, then roll and stretch out parts of you into the space into different shapes. Ready

R O L L and stretch

R O L L and stretch (many times)

3 Good. Now remember one of those shapes and run and stop in the shape.

Run and hold the shape. . .

4 Creep back to me. . .

5 Lift your arms up and down and up and down and faster until you are shaking, shaking and stop. Try again. Begin with the arms, then let the whole body move, really shaking everything. Ready. . .

6 Sit near me and listen to the music.

Yes, it goes with the shaking

And clapping?

And skipping?

7 Half of you *kneel* in a space. The other half stand behind them. Those who are kneeling, clap your hands, and shake your shoulders and toss your head — really move the body. The others step and shake and clap, travelling amongst them.

When the music fades, stand behind someone again. (Then change places.)

8 Let's make a *procession*. Everyone sit or lounge on the floor. It's a hot day in Jamaica. There's going to be a carnival procession. I will choose one of you to head a file dance. As he passes you, you get up and join him, until everyone is dancing one behind the other.

Ready - music - off you go!

9   Good, keep it going.
Now see if you can stop, and *sit one by one* on the rhythm of the music.

   sit and sit and sit and . . . (the music fades)

The Dance
A file dance or dances
Use nos. 8 and 9 many times over, encouraging development of a step pattern and shaking, shrugging shoulders and elbows.

Summary

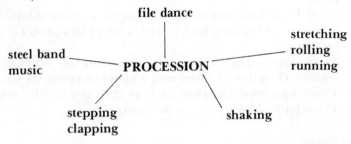

186 SKIPPING DANCE

skipping

Develop and vary according to the age and ability of the children. Young children can only cope with 'forward', 'round and round' and 'to me'. Use cupboards, walls, other children as *focuses* for change of direction. Older children can cope with more variety of direction, more precise rhythms and more arm coordination.

Accompaniment folk songs, folk dance or music James Blades, *Blades on Percussion'*.

Questions and Tasks
1   When I play the tambour, you skip; when I stop, you stop and listen. Ready, everyone skipping . . . really good skipping, stretch your back, lift your knees, use arms etc.

2 Try skipping on the spot and stop.
  Now skipping and turning on the spot.
  Now skipping forwards eight skips.
  And then turning on the spot eight skips... Keep going forwards
  and then   turning.
3 Here's a more difficult one:
    Eight skips forwards and eight skips backwards
    Four skips on the spot and four skips turning.
  Use your arms. Find an arm pattern to go with your skips.
4 Supposing you make groups of four now. How are you going to
  dance together? Make up your own skipping dance.
  Ready. . .
5 Good. I saw this group of four moving two at a time skipping to
  the centre and passing back to back without bumping. Let's all
  try that. . .
6 These three skipped around in a circle with *one* child in the
  middle. Then they changed over without stopping the dance.
  Those four used *clapping* high as they met in the centre.
  Those four added a *jump* as they met.

The Dance
A small group dance
This may evolve out of the lesson material. The movement was
directed initially to improve the skipping and coordination, and
provide directional examples. Then the children were free to discover
their own dance forms, which in turn were noted and encouraged.

Summary

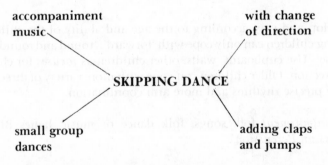

accompaniment
music

with change
of direction

SKIPPING DANCE

small group
dances

adding claps
and jumps

swing
leap
fall

Accentuate the different qualities in these movements. Work for inner involvement, energy. Choose one image to draw one of the ideas together at the end. Work from movement to imagery. Use any images that occur. Each of the actions has been developed a little. Select from the ideas.

As a *follow up,* read 'The Little Leaf Falls' from *Poems to Hear and See* by Ian Hamilton Finlay.

Questions and Tasks

1   Face your partner, well away from him, and stretch your arms to the side. Now swing *down* and up to the other side.

   Swing and swing and swing and hold high.

   Make it flow. Let the swing take you as far as it can. Bend your knees. Don't be stiff.

2   Now swing your arms towards your partner and away. Move your whole body.

   Down and forward. Down and upward.

   Like a swingboat. Keep it going, higher. Swing yourself right off the ground.

3   Now make some swings with your partner. Hold hands, then let them go . . . Swing with each other. Bring in jumps and turns.

4   Good, there are lots of different ways coming. Two there were swinging right over their heads; two there swinging down to the ground and turning.

5   Now follow your partner and do huge, war-dance *leaps* to another space and freeze. Ready, any large leaps . . .

6   Face your partner. Do a *turning leap* and hold. And turning leap and hold. Show me what sort of leap it is . . .

   Knees to the chest?

   A kick jump with the leg straight?

   You all look very fierce. Make a fierce leap dance opposite your partner . . .

7 Now, very gently, the first one *falls* to the ground, then the partner. I'll give you two sounds on the cymbal.

   And fall...

   And fall...

8 (Half the class watches. Half the class moves.) Once again, first one falls, then the partner. I want to see how many ways of falling slowly you can find.

9 Any ideas from falling?

   Leaves, aeroplanes, slow-motion diving, dying?

The Dance

A pair dance

This could be based on any one action or a combination of actions.

   One class of ten-year-olds decided on a common image of leaves falling from trees in slow motion. They performed this very beautifully, spiralling down, curling down, stretching and falling from one leg. The falling was staggered — one pair moving, then the next. (see also **137**).

Summary

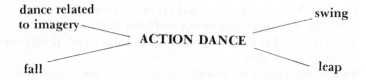

188 TUNNEL

crawl
slide
arch

The children imagine themselves in a tunnel. Different ways of *crawling* are developed, then free skipping and cartwheeling. They make a 'human tunnel' out of two files stretching towards each other making a long archway. Note how the other actions are only briefly enacted. Do not try to develop *every* aspect of the movement!

Questions and Tasks

1 Imagine you are in a tunnel. There's no room to stand up. So lie own and crawl along on your stomach. All do the same movement to start with. Tuck one leg up beside you, the other one stretched out very straight behind you. Have one hand near your shoulder, one hand stretched out in front. Really stretch. . .

   Now crawl. Bend and stretch the legs and arms. Really work the arms, the legs, the back.

2 OK you are out of the tunnel. Flop out on the ground for a moment.

3 Try going along the tunnel again. Try other ways of getting along this tunnel — big movements. Ready and . . .

4 Good. Let's pick out some of these. This one, on hands and feet. See how he brings his feet right up to his hands. Then pulling himself along, sliding on his tummy.

5 You're *out of* the tunnel! Move into the spaces. You can do all sorts of movement now when you're out of the tunnel. You can skip, cartwheel — choose your movement.

6 Everyone sit. How can we make a human tunnel? Suggestions?

7 The first two go and stand at the end of the room facing each other, well apart. Stretch your hands overhead to meet to make an arch. The next two go and make your arch in front of them. Good, your arch is kneeling, stretching sideways to meet. (And so on until the whole class has made a tunnel which is really two files with partners opposite one another and stretching towards each other in a variety of ways.)

The Dance

Half the class makes tunnels, the other half travels through them. Change over. Unison 'happy movement' to end.

   Alternatively, each group makes a tunnel. The first two children travel through the tunnel and then join on the end of it. The next two travel through, and so on, until all the children in the group have travelled through.

   The tunnel collapses.

Summary

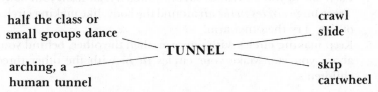

half the class or small groups dance		crawl slide
	TUNNEL	
arching, a human tunnel		skip cartwheel

Movement Patterns

189 CIRCLES

circling
running

Circles can stimulate circling *body parts*, a circle *floor pattern* or a
circle *formation*. Use a brightly-coloured circle pattern or design as a
stimulus.

Accompaniment pre-recorded 'humming' at different pitches and
phrase lengths.
(See Conducting voice sounds, **50**.)

Questions and Tasks
Formation
1   In groups of four, hold hands very lightly, elbows a little bent.
    Rise up on your toes and let's see which group can *run* in a very
    smooth circle. Do it to the sounds we recorded. As the sound
    fades, slow down and stop.
2   Try the other way, holding very lightly, hardly touching. Ready,
    running lightly . . . and stop.

Floor pattern
3   Now each one of you run a circle *on the floor* and back to your
    own space as if you are making a circle of footprints.

Body parts
4   Each one of you hold out your *arm*, stretch it far from your body.
    Trace huge *circles in the air* around the body, like making circles
    of fire. Try the other arm.
5   Keep making circles with one arm, then the other, behind you,
    above you etc. Make your circles *fit in* with the other three
    children's.

6   Make a circling idea together. You could use your leg or your head.

That was a lovely idea. His head circled down to the ground as her arms circled *over* him.

7   How many ways can each group find of making a circle? Every time I *tap the drum* make a different circle formation.

Good. I saw:

a back-to-back circle

a circle lying on the floor, feet in the centre

a circle falling with arms high (etc.)

The Dance

In groups of four

Titles like magic circles, fire circles, flying saucers, hoops might arise. Give a framework of beginning and ending in circle formation to a certain length of humming.

Younger children could work with the teacher in two groups — a circle formation with a group inside it. Alternate travelling *around* the circle with circling body parts inside it.

Summary

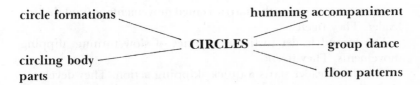

circle formations

humming accompaniment

CIRCLES

group dance

circling body parts

floor patterns

190 KALEIDOSCOPE

moving
stopping

Look down a kaleidoscope. See how the particles move and stop in different shapes and patterns. Use the idea of moving in different ways; stopping in different ways.

Accompaniment a tambourine to stimulate the shaking of the kaleidoscope.

Questions and Tasks

1 Stand by yourself in a space. Listen to the tambourine. Roll and balance high in any *shape* you like. And again.

2 *Skipping* and turning amongst each other. Use lots of changes of direction — in and out, up and down. And *still*. Try that many times. Every time you stop, you form a *pattern* with someone near you.

3 Take a partner's hand. Move with your partner on the spot. Move up and down, under arms, round each other, get twisted up together. Make a pattern together. And stop and shake yourselves apart.

4 Are there any more ideas based on what you saw in the kaleidoscope? Try travelling slowly. Now travel along amongst each other with *sharp* movements as if your knees, elbows or feet were made of sharp glass. Move and stop with the tambourine.

5 Practise sharp jumps with the fingers shooting high. Practise that sharp knee in the air, turn.

The Dance

A dance for three

The children intermingle and freeze. Each child in turn acts as a leader for the sort of travelling the group does.

The group moves with sharp accented movements around the first leader. They freeze.

The second leader instigates a series of slow turning, dipping movements. They freeze.

The third leader starts a quick skipping action. They develop a circle floor pattern.

The dance ends with the children sinking gently down into a variety of body shapes.

In each part of the dance the children should have a clear relationship to each other.

Summary

tambourine   group dances   (moving, stopping into shapes)

KALEIDOSCOPE

travel slowly, sharply

twist   skip   roll, balance

curving
twisting
and giant steps

'It looks like a *rainbow*.'
'It looks like huge, different-colour *snakes*.'
'All different *patterns* together.'
'It's like giant *footprints*.'

Immediately after a dance lesson, a group of six-year-olds painted a large, brilliantly-coloured 'moving painting', which was full of swirls, blobs and zig-zag patterns. Their remarks about it (above) were used as the stimulus for the next dance lesson.

Accompaniment Flute Sonata, Poulenc from *Listen, Move & Dance*

Questions and Tasks

1   Who can make a rainbow shape of his body? A rainbow *curves*. All stand with your feet together and your arms stretched high overhead, and bend one way and the other way.

   And bend and bend and . . .

2   How else can we make a curve? Yes, from *kneeling*, curve backwards and then *curl* in forwards. Make a big rainbow backwards and curl forwards.

3   Hold your hand high. Now imagine you are painting those enormous coloured *snakes*. Paint them in the air all around the body. Ready . . .

   'Up and down and to the side and behind you and to the floor... Big twisting movements. Keep painting the air full of snakes. And still.

4   Try once again. This time sometimes use *one hand*, sometimes the other. Try to go high and low.

5   Now half of you (i.e. half the class) stand still in your space. The other half are going to travel in amongst you twisting, turning, making snake patterns on the floor. Ready . . .

6 Now the other half. This time the ones who are on the spot move their *arms*, snake arms. The ones who are *moving* about use up and down as well as in and out — all moving and curving, snake arms, snake feet.

7 Lie in your space and stick a *giant foot* up in the air. Make it go as high as it can. And put it down. And the other giant foot. Good. Now sit up and make yourself as wide as you can, stretch your arms.

Relax.

8 As I point to you, stand up and come to me with *giant steps*. Ready . . .

And *walk, walk, walk, walk* ...

And ...

The Dance
A short individual dance
This could evolve in a subsequent lesson as 'My Curly Dance' to Flute Sonata by Poulenc *(Listen, Move and Dance)*. Older children could make partner or small-group dances based on curving air and floor patterns.

Summary

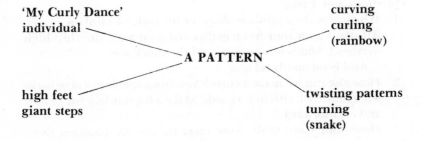

Objects

192 THE BALL

bounce
spin
roll

Note the development used in this lesson and compare it to 'Bounce and spin' (223) and 'Magic sound' (227) lessons where the same root actions are used with different development. This is the way movement progresses.

Remember here to use the *looking* at the ball as an initial stimulus. Do not dance to the ball's movement. This is too limiting. Make it clear to the children when they are to come to you and when to stay in place.

Follow up make a collection of things that bounce, spin or roll (e.g. marbles, sycamore seeds).

Questions and Tasks

1 Watch the ball carefully. Whatever it does I want you to do. Don't *tell* me, *show* me with your body. (The teacher bounces the ball.) Spread out quickly . . . Ready and . . .

2 How many ideas did you have? I'll bounce the ball and then you begin . . .

3 Good, I saw high and low bounces and some people turning *and* bouncing.
   Try again. It might be a strange ball that goes tremendously high.

4 Sit on the floor. Now watch (spin it and *stop* it). Ready, off you go.

5 We had spinning on your *seat* but you could stretch your legs much more.
   And spinning on *one leg*. Can you lift and stretch the other one? Everyone practise that one.
   Spin on one leg (to the right) and
   Spin on one leg (to the left).

6   And what else can the ball do? (Roll the ball.) Everyone begin to move a slow-motion *roll*. Really slow.

7   What can your *legs* do as you roll? That is a very good idea. All try . . . Start on your knees, roll onto your back. Stretch your legs in the air, curl up and roll onto your knees. Again . . . (i.e. clarify and develop the skill).

The Dance

'Make your own "Ball dance". Use bouncing, spinning, rolling. Use other ideas you have thought of. What happens to you in the end?'

This idea arouses great enthusiasm. The older the child the more the stress is laid on combining actions. Fantasy could develop: the ball might have a magic power — everyone caught up in bionic bounces. Use the lesson's movement content as a guide.

Summary

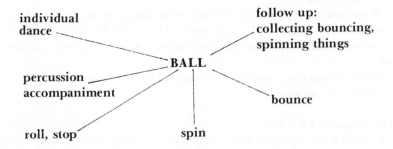

individual dance

follow up: collecting bouncing, spinning things

BALL

percussion accompaniment

roll, stop

spin

bounce

193 (a) BALLOON

grow
bounce, burst
drift, settle

A variety of actions arise from *watching* a balloon. Watch the balloon and then make a rhythmic accompaniment with voice or percussion to practise phrases of action. The lesson demonstrates how the children's response is used in the development of the ideas.

Accompaniment tambourine and cymbal.

Questions and Tasks

1 Listen to the sound, Start curled up and show me how you grow bigger and bigger and bigger and then smaller again. Lots of times.

2 Begin by balancing on any part of yourself. Can you grow much bigger this time? Perhaps your *leg* grows out a long way into the space behind you. Yes, all different-shaped ones.

3 Let's watch the balloon (inflated), and see how it goes along. Yes, it's *bouncing* very lightly. Half of you sit down in a space. The other half are going to bounce in the spaces amongst you.
   The sitting ones, bounce your *fingertips* on the floor. Ready . . . (then change over).

4 Someone there was bouncing with legs wide apart. Could you all bounce in different shapes like different-shaped balloons?

5 Now everyone in a space, show me any balloon shape. Let the balloon sway a little, very gently.
   Now I'm going to
      BURST you!
   Let's try that again. You burst very suddenly, and you land up still. Ready . . .

6 Good, some people are leaping, spinning or collapsing as they burst. Who is going to show us their bursting action?

7 Now start near me. You're my bunch of balloons - all different shapes. You're so light I am going to *blow you* away. As I blow you, *drift* into a space and settle there. (Blow a few at a time.)

8 Now slowly, slowly, I let your air out . . .down you go, gently to the ground.

The Dance

The children can provide a simple story framework — perhaps:
   The balloons are blown up lots of times before they stay up.
   They bounce gently around the room.
   They burst and all the pieces lie still.
Older children enjoy stretching into balloon shapes with a partner so that the movement is continuous, involving balancing, arching and rolling skills. One partner can inflate the other one!
   The *sound* a balloon makes as it rapidly deflates, and the movement of travelling quickly (with rolling, tumbling or turning) to another spot, might also be used.

Summary

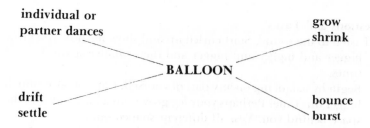

individual or
partner dances

grow
shrink

BALLOON

drift
settle

bounce
burst

193(b) DANCING WITH A BALLOON

toss
float
run
leap

Dance *with* the balloon here. Attach balloons to short lengths of string. Demonstrate with one or two children how to hold the balloon firmly *far* from the body, so the body is stretched. Stress the use of the back. The balloon must be *followed* by the body stretching, bending and twisting. Stress the *quality* of the balloon.

Have a group moving at a time.

Accompaniment Tubular Bells — Mike Oldfield.

Questions and Tasks

1   Hold your balloon far from you to one side. Now *toss* it lightly upwards (keep hold of the string) and let it float down, then *toss* it again.

Toss. . . and float, and toss . . . and float.

2   Make your whole body go upwards as you toss, and then sink down. Follow the movement of the balloon.

3   Good, I saw a knee and hand toss upwards too. Make the whole body join in. Try toss and float now with the music. As the music fades, sink downwards.

4   Space well out. Hold the balloon in your hands. Now throw it up gently and catch it gently. Sink downwards with the balloon. Feel how light it is. (Each group has a turn.)

5   Now throw it, turn under it and catch it.
    Throw . . . turn and catch.
    or
    Turn, clap and catch. Try not to let the balloon touch the ground.

6   Good, I can see some lovely, *smooth* sequences of movement.

7   Half of you sit by the wall. The other half spread out and all go round *this* way. I want you to *run* smoothly with the balloon held high above your head.

8   Now the second half try. Can you add a light leap to the running?
    Run run leap. Run run leap.

The Dance

1   *An individual dance* to music.
    Show me how your dance begins. Show me where it goes in the space and how it ends.

2   *Partners* who must 'share' one balloon, one still and one moving
    or
    one dancing with the balloon and one 'echoing' the movement. Another idea is to keep the balloon high by tapping it up gently with the hand, elbow, knee, head etc.

Summary

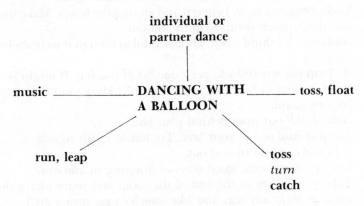

individual or
partner dance

music ———————— DANCING WITH ———— toss, float
A BALLOON

run, leap   toss
                                                  turn
                                                  catch

129

lift, skip
crouch, peep
jump
travel in

Use short, controlled phrases. Stress moving carefully. Half the class moves at a time. A story idea may develop.

Accompaniment drumming, or quiet jazz for older children.

Questions and Tasks
1   Lift the box *high* above your head and *place it down* beside you, high above and place it down the other side. Treat it like something precious. Bend and stretch as you move it.
2   Could you go into a *shoulder stand* and lift the box up on your feet, and bring it down again without it falling off?
3   Light skipping now, between and around the boxes. Make sure you don't touch them. Skip in and out.
4   And *crouch behind* a box. Hide behind as though it were sheltering you.
5   As I tap the woodblock, *peep* one bit of you out. It might be a *hand*, a *head*, a *foot* that comes out of hiding, and then goes back in again.
6   And *JUMP* out from behind your box.
7   *Jump in* and *out* of your box. Try not to touch it, and
     In and out and in and out.
    Let's work on some good ways of jumping in and out.
8   Take your boxes to the end of the room and move along the room *in them* any way you like (one foot in, sitting etc.)

The Dance

A half-the-class dance

The first half dances with the boxes. Each child makes his own dance with a clear beginning and ending. Then they change over. Make the dance short, to a definite length of music. A little story may result.

The idea of 'hiding' behind boxes was also used in a 'Pied Piper' idea. The rats hid and peeped out.

Summary

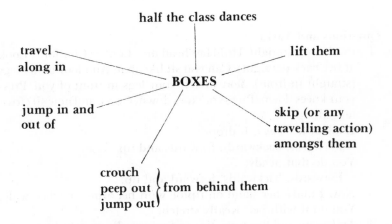

half the class dances

travel along in

lift them

BOXES

jump in and out of

skip (or any travelling action) amongst them

crouch peep out jump out } from behind them

195 CHARLOTTE and JIMMY

Charlotte is a floppy rag doll, and Jimmy is a simple jointed marionette — pull the string and his legs fly up.

flop, stretch swing, tiptoe jump

The above are very useful stimuli for a wide age range. Obviously the tone of this lesson is aimed at young children. Juniors have enjoyed finding all the strange movements and positions that Charlotte uses. In this lesson she is used for sitting with straight backs and for *extending* arms and legs, as well as being a creative stimulus for floppy movements.

Accompaniment young children - percussion — older children — music

Questions and Tasks

1 (Sit her up straight. Hold her head up.) Look at Charlotte. Look at her back (straight). Can you sit like that? And look at her legs (straight in front). You stretch your legs in front of you. Press your knees down. Press your toes down. Good, and now sit cross-legged.

2 Look at her *head*. It drops
   Forwards, backwards, forwards and up.
   You do that, ready:
   Forwards, backwards, forward and up. . .

3 Now I make her stand on tiptoe with her arms stretched wide. You do it with her. Really stretch.

4 And again and this time, tiptoe, tiptoe really stretched into your space . . . And sit on the floor.

5 Now Charlotte's going to dance for you. (Make the doll dance.) Yes, she's *swinging* her legs and *flopping* her head (etc.). See how she stops. Yes, she's got her leg over her ear.

6 Everyone show me a floppy starting position. Now listen to the tambourine play:
   Floppety, shaky, shaky, flop sounds and you dance. Ready . . .

7 Those were lovely dances. I saw feet flopping up, and arms flopping round, Let's all practise floppy backs . . . and floppy hands . . . and floppy legs.

8 Now half the class sit here by me and half the class find a starting position and show us your floppy dance. What funny position are you going to end in? (Change over.)

9 All sit near me. Look, here's Jimmy. What's he doing? Jumping his legs wide apart in the air. Everyone stand. Spread a little way away from me. Watch Jimmy and do four big *jumps* with him. Ready . . . and flop down to sitting. A floppy sit. And now a straight-backed sit.

The Dance

The individual dance

This evolved in nos. 5-8. Older children would of course work on the dance longer and in more detail. Jimmy could be a starting point for *different* kinds of jumps (the ones Jimmy can't do as well as the ones he can!) in another lesson.

Summary

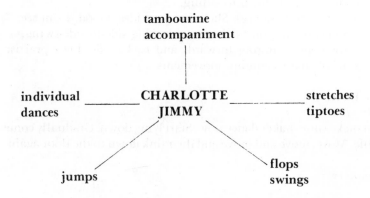

196 CRÊPE PAPER SHAKER

shake
fly
swing
settle

Watch what it does. Move it for the children. Practise one idea at a time. Practise variations of each action. (The shaker could also be danced *with* see **76**.)

Accompaniment tambourine

Questions and Tasks
1 Watch it (shaking). You make a dance like that.
2 Good. We had *shaking* feet, hands etc. Everyone shake your hands high in the air and low near the ground.
3 Now watch it *fly* from one space . . . to another. Everyone stand, lift your heads up high, and *FLY* to another space, and *FLY* again and sink down to sitting.
4 Now watch it *(swing)*. Show me your idea. Good. I can see:
   Someone ther on his knees with a big side-to-side swing.
   Someone swinging forwards and backwards. Let's practise some of those swinging movements.

The Dance
Individual
You make your shaker dance now. Start lying down. Gradually come to life. Move, move and move and then sink down to the floor again.

Summary

individual dance   shake high and low

SHAKER

swing   fly

197 ELASTIC

stretch
curl up
vibrate
pull

Make the elastic move. Encourage the children to watch and copy the quality of the elastic. Later on they could move with it, stretching and pulling, joined to a partner.

Questions and Tasks

1 Watch how it stretches and stretches and curls up quickly.
2 Stretch the whole of yourself as far as you can and curl up quickly. Again . . . Try this from standing. Now from lying.
3 Watch how I stretch it up into the air.
4 Lie down. Whichever part of your body I call, you are going to stretch that part up into the air . . .
   Your arm! Knee and hand! One foot! Two feet!
5 Now you choose which part. Ready . . .
6 Now stride with stretching steps. Move fast. Really stretch your legs to the rhythm.
7 All follow this boy. Stride, stride, stride, stride. Now all follow this girl.
8 Stay in your space. Stretch towards me. Can you balance on one foot? Stretch and let go.
9 Come close to me. Stretch away, more and more and *collapse*. Again. . .
10 Watch the elastic *vibrate*. I make it vibrate up and down.
11 Standing, make your hands vibrate, shiver, shake; your shoulders, your middles.
12 Shake yourselves down to the floor fast and shake and vibrate as much as you can. And still.
13 Half the class moves, trembles, vibrates from standing to lying to sitting, while the other half makes trembling voice sounds with me to accompany. Notice those who move every part of themselves.
14 All sit in a line facing me. As I beat the drum, run and stretch one by one, behind or beside the other, so that you make a long, stretchy line like a long piece of elastic.
15 Now everyone begin to tremble and collapse, roll away and lie still.
16 Lie very still. As I touch you, stand slowly.

The Dance

Unison class dance or individual dance

A sequence of actions could be selected from the above ideas, and chosen after discussion. Numbers 13 or 14 could be repeated over and over again to make a satisfying culmination to the lesson. Partner work could be developed from many of the examples.

Summary

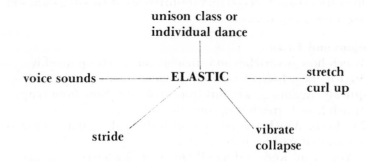

unison class or
individual dance

voice sounds ———————— ELASTIC ————— stretch
curl up

stride

vibrate
collapse

198 FLOPPY FROG

flop
stretch
jump

With the children gathered round watching, the teacher moves a bean-bag frog, using one movement idea at a time. The children space out and try the idea, then gather round and watch again. The frog is the starting point for invention and is not meant to be copied exactly. (see also Things **202**).

Follow up talking and frog words (see Flash cards **58-65**).

Questions and Tasks

1 Watch what he does. I pick him up and drop him down. Yes, he is *flopping* down. Can you do that? Find a space. *Stretch* up high and *flop* down. And again. Really *stretch* hard, really *flop*.

2 Come back to me. Watch what he *looks* like on the floor after I've dropped him. Yes, he is in a funny *shape* - his legs are over his head, one arm is spread out (etc.) . . .
Show me your floppy shape on the floor. Now *stretch* up high and *flop* down and show me another floppy shape.

3 Come back to me. Watch how I lift him off the floor by his *toe* or his *head* etc. I make his toe *stretch* in the air and *flop* down again. Make your floppy shape on the floor. Whichever *part* of you I call out, you *stretch* it up into the air and *flop* it down again.

4 Now he's tired of being on one spot. What is he doing? Yes, *jumping* from one space to another space all over the room. You do that. Ready . . .
Let's practise some ways of jumping.

The Dance
A little story
Frog is always trying to get off the ground and jump high, but he always flops back down again. (Or perhaps one day he succeeds and *jumps* away.)

Choose from some of the above ideas and accompany the action story with voice and percussion. Stress a clear beginning and ending.

Summary

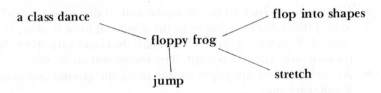

a class dance

flop into shapes

floppy frog

jump

stretch

199 LEAF

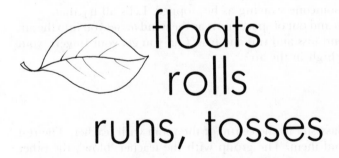

floats
rolls
runs, tosses

This lesson has two main contrasts: in place/travel and sudden/sustained.

Accompaniment tambourine or voice sound.

Questions and Tasks

1   Sit near me. Watch the leaf as I let go of it. (Toss it in the air.)
    What does it do? Yes, it floats or falls down.
    It goes this way and that way.
2   Kneeling, everyone stretch you fingers high and then *down* they
    come -
        this way, that way,
        this way, that way,
        touch the ground and stretch up again.
    Try it again lots of times. Make your body move with your hands.
3   As I point to you, find a space and show me a big stretch up in the
    air as if you're hanging from a branch . . .
4   Now altogether, listen to the cymbal (a quiet tap) and *float*
    down to the ground and up again.
5   This time, float your fingers down, follow your fingers *one side,
    the other side.*
    When you reach the ground, roll right over and up again.
    Ready ... And float, float down and *roll* and stretch up again and
    float . . .
6   Can you walk back to me on tiptoe and sit down very softly?
7   Watch the leaf. I'm going to be the wind and blow it *along the
    ground.* Watch what it does. Then half the class find a space; lie
    on your side, closed up tight. The rest of you sit by me.
8   As we blow, you are going to roll along the ground and stop.
    Ready with me . . .
    Blow-w-w-w-w, and still. Now we are going to blow you *back* to
    where you started from. Ready . . .
    (change groups and repeat).
9   I saw someone swaying as he stopped. Let's all try that.
10 Run in and out of spaces now as the wind *tosses* you into the air.
    Run and toss and run and toss. Can you get your fingers, your
    knees, high in the air?

The Dance

Half the class sits in the centre of the room with teacher. The rest
spread round them. The group with the teacher 'blow', the other
children dance.

   They float up and down on the spot, then run and toss to another
   space and settle on the ground.

Make a clear framework of sound for the above. (See also Swing,
leap, fall, **187.**)

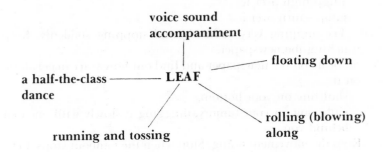

voice sound
accompaniment

a half-the-class —— **LEAF** —— floating down
dance

running and tossing rolling (blowing) along

200 NEWSPAPER

balance on
jump over
travel on

Try to encourage sensitivity to touching the newspaper with different body parts while balancing on the newspaper, and then a variety of ideas for ways of travelling on it. The *sound* the newspaper makes could be included in the idea. Stress choosing *one* main idea for the dance.

Questions and Tasks
1 Sit very still on your piece of newspaper.
2 Move slowly and carefully
   onto your knees
   then to standing
   then down to sitting again.
   (Listen to the slow beat on the tambour.)
3 Find out how many ways you can *balance* on your newspaper. Keep changing your position, moving slowly. (Yes, it is like being on a raft.)

4   Now stand beside your paper, and jump over it.
    Jump high over it
    jump - turn over it
    Try jumping very suddenly and stopping suddenly. Keep watching the newspaper.

5   Sit or lie on the newspaper and find out how you can get along on it:
    shuffling on your bottom
    slithering on your tummy, dragging it slowly with one foot behind you.
    Keep the movement going. Stop when the tambour stops. Let's all practise some of the ways you have discovered.

6   For a moment, you decide on any other ways of using it. Start when I tap the tambour. Stop when I tap it again. Good.
    Jumping on to it
    screwing it up so it makes loud sounds
    wearing it on your head.

7   One by one, put your piece of newspaper in a pile in the centre of the room.

The Dance
Small group dances
A dance could be built around three action words:
balance on it
move over and around it
screw it up and leave it.

Or the newspaper 'becomes' something - a raft, quicksands. This will be suggested by the nature of the movement.

Summary
Accompaniment tambour, silence, newspaper, sounds.

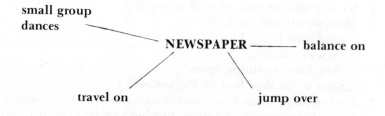

skip steps
tossing, twisting
hopping

The rope is used in the hands around the body and placed on the floor to stimulate a variety of movements. Stress qualitative movement, the relationship *with* the rope.

Accompaniment Kodaly 'Dances of Galanta' 2 ACL 75 or any simple skipping tune. Tossing and twisting could have tambourine accompaniment.

Questions and Tasks

1   Half the class sit by me. Half find a space. *Skip on the spot* with your rope. Listen to the music. Use the rhythm. Try different skipping steps. (Change over.)
2   Now make *combinations* of steps as you skip. Use turning as well. (Change over.)
3   Good. There were lots of different *sequences* then.
4   Everyone *fold* your rope in half and hold it, so that the two ends are together.
5   Try *tossing and moving* the rope *around* the body, so you stretch and bend and turn. Keep it moving, up, down and behind you.
6   Try moving it with the other hand.
    Try from kneeling.
    See what different body *shapes* the rope makes you move into.
7   Put the rope *down on the floor* in a straight line. With your partner, *follow my leader* down the rope, jumping from one side to the other.
8   That was a very good step. All try that:
    Step hop, jump the feet apart, jump, land on one foot.

The Dance

A half-the-class dance

Put a pile of ropes in the middle of the room. One by one, the children take one and find a space.

They begin to toss the rope in the space around the body, *twisting and turning*, rising and sinking.

As the music comes up they begin to use the rope to *skip* with. The music fades.

They slowly place the rope down on the floor. They then lightly bounce and *jump* over the ropes back to the teacher.

The second group goes one by one to a rope and repeats the idea.

Alternatively, a partner dance might evolve.

Summary

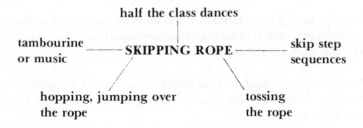

202 THINGS

This works best with children who have some background in dance. One object is explored briefly as an example. Then each group is given an object (not the shell — see no. 3 below) and asked to make a short dance. The teacher has to observe and develop the movement response (see **71, 72**.)

Questions and Tasks

1   Come and look at these things I've brought along. Now start near me. As I tap the woodblock, I want you to run into a space and make yourself into the shape of one of the objects. See if I can guess which one you are doing.

2   This time, make the shapes really large so I can see where your legs are (where you head is) in the space.
Ready, run and freeze. Good, masses of different ones there, some balanced on their feet, some on their shoulders.

3   Come and sit near me. Have a look at this *shell*. Yes, it's sharp with bits sticking out all over it. Could you grow slowly into that shape?

4   Curl up in a space and listen to the tambour. *Press* your arms, hands, feet, away from you into a balance. Press yourself into a *large, spiked* shape. And sink down again. And again . . . press, press . . .

5   How would you move along in that shape? As if the shell is being moved along by waves? That's a good idea. Turning from hand to knee, to seat, to hand, on the floor, stretching up the other parts of you as you roll and turn.
(All try several ways.)

6   Each group now has an object. Put it in the middle of your group and spread out round it. Now all of you, show me a starting position that your object suggests to you. Good . . . and rest. And once again your starting position.

7   Now move in any way that your object suggests to you. What *actions* are you using? What *shapes* do you move into?

The Dance

Give a specific time length (five minutes) for the dance to be worked on. Help each group to clarify and improve the actions and shapes that evolve. Stress flow, keeping the movement going.
   One group used the 'frog'. They played with it and made it *move*:
leaping
lying down, fling the legs over the head
spin on the stomach etc.
and then evolved a flowing sequence of unison actions.
   (Any one of these objects could of course be taken separately as a lesson idea.)

Group dances
These evolved from the actions, shapes and rhythms of the 'things'.

Summary

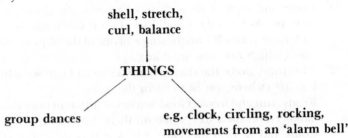

shell, stretch,
curl, balance

THINGS

group dances

e.g. clock, circling, rocking,
movements from an 'alarm bell'

Dressing Up

203 CLOAKS

open
whirl
close

The 'cloak' is a square of material held in the hands passing behind the back so that it is taut when the arms are stretched. The idea of handling and moving with a cloak can be introduced in the classroom. One or two children can try out the idea.

Divide the class into four equal groups. In this lesson the children move *without* the cloaks and then with them. This degree of control may not of course be necessary.

Accompaniment tambour or music - Granados 'Spanish Dance-Andaluza'.

Questions and Tasks

1 Everyone in a space. Stand with your arms as wide as you can, as if you are holding out an enormous cloak - very stretched, very proud and lifted.

2 Now imagine you are wrapping a cloak around you. Wrap your arms around you, close up. Bend your knees, tuck your head in and then *open* wide again.

> And *wide* and close *in*,
> and wide and close in . . .

   Use big movements.

3 Now step very deep, closing your cloak round you low near the ground, and then open out as you step *high*. Listen to the rhythm. Ready . . .

4   Who can bend right *back*? Curve back with your cloak wide and then *forward* to kneeling, closing the cloak round you.
    Move with cloaks, one group at a time. One group sits about the room, well spaced out. The second group dances among them with the cloaks. The cloaks are then handed to the second group-handed very ceremoniously as part of the movement.
5   The children try the opening and closing movement with their cloaks. Make a dance with the cloak. Try:
    opening
    closing in
    swirling round
    using high and low.
6   Good. I saw some people really stretching, moving very smoothly using big movements. (Groups change over.)
7   The next group might try *whirling* the cloak around the body, or *running* with the cloak flying behind them.

The Dance

1   *A partner dance*
    One moving near, one still. Changing over the cloak. The stillness could be in a variety of positions. Perhaps the cloak 'brings you to life'. Many other partner ideas are possible. The relationship between the two can be evolved by the children or set as a limitation by the teacher.

2   *In a circle, sitting*
    A quarter of the class are in the centre - statues ready to move, holding the cloaks. The children sitting clap softly and rhythmically. The children in the centre dance. The clapping fades. The children gently leave the cloaks on the ground and move quietly back into the circle. The teacher calls out the names of the next children to dance.

Summary

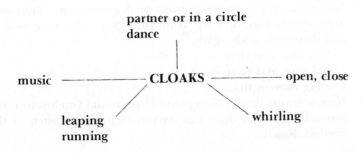

partner or in a circle
dance

music ———————— CLOAKS ———————— open, close

leaping
running

whirling

People

204 CLOWNS

walk
balance
run
fall

It is particularly important in this dance to stress rhythmic movement, and give both short phrases of action and short lengths of time for practising.

Quick line drawings of clowns balancing in different shapes on different parts of their bodies help to stimulate inventiveness. Funny shapes could also be employed in jumping. The main emphasis here is that clown-like movement can be developed without resource to mime, although the 'custard-pie' movement might well be a unison action which would draw the whole class together at the end.

Accompaniment percussion or a march e.g. a march by Sousa.

Follow up make red noses out of cardboard egg-box sections and elastic, or make huge, newspaper-collage clowns, by tearing newspaper and making it into clown shapes in different positions.

Questions and Tasks
1   Ready! Four walks on your heels. Four walks on your toes. Can you do that lots of times? Listen to the rhythm.
2   Show me another funny walk. Yes, with your toes turned in and your toes turned out. Altogether now . . . (perhaps knees high - swinging arms).
3   Look at this picture of a clown. Yes, he's balancing on his bottom with his legs in the air. Show me!

4   Stand up. Every time I hit the cymbal you show me a clown balance. Ready . . .
5   There's a good one. Everyone try a balance on their front with their arms and legs lifted behind. Now roll over into another balance. Try a balance on one leg.
6   Ready! Run and balance and again. Run and balance.
7   There was an interesting one. Everyone run with knees high. Run, run and balance. Run with nose high . . .
8   Stand opposite your partner. Fall and balance. Take turns. See if you can make your balance different from your partner's. Jump up again after you have fallen.
9   All practise your clown movement - walking, balancing, falling and balancing. Begin when I tap the woodblock. Finish when I tap it again.
10 Everyone stay quite still in your balance. This boy is going to tiptoe amongst you. As he taps you, join on the end of his line.
11 Let's have a follow-my-leader clown file to end - walking with noses and knees high.

The Dance
1 *A simple class dance*
A class dance might be developed from nos. 9, 10 and 11 ending with a file of follow-my-leader clowns. Alternatively the dance could involve partners rather than individuals. Older children enjoy moving in unison, building a short sequence.
2 *Walking and falling*
Use walking sounds and falling sounds as the framework of a dance. Half the class could play instruments and the other half move; or one half could be walking clowns and one half falling clowns.

Summary

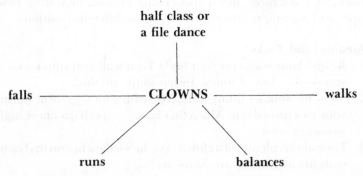

148

creep
roll
leap

This lesson contains many movement ideas. An initial lesson could rough out the idea and subsequent lessons concentrate on the individual development of body parts, shape and sequence making. It would be a mistake with most age groups to attempt to explore each part in detail. Individual creativity might contrast with unison movements selected by the teacher.

Accompaniment music Red Indian
Follow up making head-dresses with elastic, feathers and beads.

Questions and Tasks

1   Here come the Indians creeping, and STILL, Shhh ... Creeping again.
2   Listen to the woodblock. Freeze absolutely still when the sound stops.
3   Which direction are you creeping in?
4   Everyone now practise creeping to the side - one, two, three and backwards, backwards, backwards.
5   Can we do that again, but creep really low with big creeps this time?
6   Now try creeping high, then low. Listen. I'll give you a very short time to creep high *and* low.
7   Quick. Everyone roll, roll and still. Yes, it's like getting away from danger.
    Again roll, roll and still.
    What sort of roll were you doing?
8   All try that stretched-out one. Show me how you stop.
9   Now, all the boys run very fast to another space and STOP. Ready! Now the girls. Ready! Repeat. Use running and leaping this time.
10 Sit on the floor now and listen to the sound of the drum. The drum is calling you through the forest.

11 You make up your journey through the forest. Sometimes creep, sometimes roll, sometimes run and leap. Stop and listen often.

12 I saw some people go really fast, then really slowly. Show me where your movement goes faster and then very slow.

13 Come to me now and say the Indian 'Hello'. All shout 'How!' Now all leap and stop strongly, pressing your hands into the air. Say 'How!' as you leap.

14 Half the class leaps and say 'How!' Then the other half.

15 All make one large circle. Skip strongly around, beating your feet on the floor. What should your arms do?

16 Let's all make the same arm action, and the same foot rhythm.

17 How shall the movement end? All right, stretch your arms into the air and sink down to kneeling.

The Dance
Individually, the Indians creep and roll and run through the forest. At a signal they run into groups and greet each other with a leap and a 'How!' Ceremonial circle dances end the dance. This idea involves individual creativity in the first part and a group *unison* action in the second part.

Summary

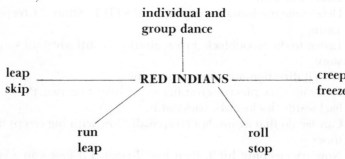

206 WITCHES

twist
shoot

This dance is based on one main action - TWIST - which is explored through a variety of developments. Care must be taken to vary the

speed and pace of the different movement experiences and compens-
atory movements of shooting or shaking provided to release any
tension.

Accompaniment a witches' chant or music — Falla, *Ritual Fire
Dance* from El Amor Brujo.

Follow up making costumes and masks.

Questions and Tasks
1   Sit near me. Twist your hands into a twisted shape. Listen to the
    woodblock and change the shape. Shoot your fingers into the
    air.
2   Can you twist the wrists, the fingers, the whole arm, the body, so
    you are very twisted all over?
3   Standing, try the same idea now, twisting *quickly* into different
    shapes. Use your hands, use your whole body.
    Ready and twist!
    Then shoot the arms upwards.
4   Find your own space and practise this idea. You change your
    shape now when *you* decide.
5   I saw some people twisting from high to low. Let's all try that.
    And from low to high. Try to finish with one hand low, one
    hand high.
6   All practise that twisting jump into the air.
7   Look for a space and travel into it along a twisting, turning
    pathway. Don't go straight there. Go this way, that way, this
    way.
8   Can you make your arms and legs twist and turn as you travel
    along?
9   Half the class stands in a twisted shape. Now the other half twists
    and travels amongst them . . . fast and stop.
10 Sit near me. Let's make up a *spell*, a very short one we can all say
    together. Move your hands as you say it.

The Dance
1 *A witches' circle*
Use music for the dance. The children begin crouched in a
circle. One by one they rise from the ground into twisted shapes.
Then intermingle, fitting in together, contrasting high and
low movement. (Fade music.) The return to their places in
the circle and begin a repetitive chant accompanied by a unison

action (to symbolize pot-stirring, or making a spell). This grows to a climax and a suitable action ending is devised, for example 'disappearing' with a leap and a fall.

2 *Voice sounds*

A witches' chant can accompany the movement. Initially practise the chant separately. Not all children are capable of moving and sounding simultaneously. They may lose all movement clarity. Younger and less-experienced children would do better to use the chant only as an introduction or culmination of the main movement idea.

Summary

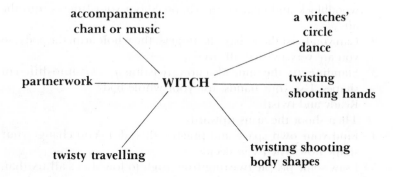

accompaniment: chant or music

a witches' circle dance

partnerwork —————— WITCH —————— twisting shooting hands

twisty travelling

twisting shooting body shapes

Moods

207   ANGER

stamp
leap
hit

Accompaniment cymbal and drum. Use crescendo and decrescendo
(see also **90**).

Follow up Masks can be useful additions to the dance. Make them
out of cardboard plates. (See useful books, page **224**.)

Questions and Tasks
1   Show me a really angry face. What do your eyes, jaw (etc.) look
    like? Change it and show me another angry face. Every time I tap
    the woodblock, change your face.
2   Stand slowly and make your whole body look angry. How does
    your body feel? Yes, very strong.
3   Change your position and with two big stamps show me strong
    legs, strong arms, strong head.
        stamp stamp hold
        stamp stamp hold.
    Try to make the strong shapes different.
4   Run and leap high with an angry face and body. Stop very still
    after your leap and hold your position. (Try half the class at a
    time.)
        Run and *leap* and
        run and leap.
5   Find a partner and leap one after the other. Show me some
    strong-leap shapes. See if you can finish in a different position
    from your partner.
6   Spread out and hold your right arm very wide. Now make one
    big hitting movement. Now another. Now two together. Do the
    same with the left arm. Work on a sequence using hit, leap and
    stamp.

7 Stand in a strong position and then gradually relax until you are sitting gently.

The Dance
An individual or partner dance
Try making an Angry dance which begins slowly and gathers speed and strength to a climax, using the actions explored. The conclusion? A gentle sinking down, or a quiet return to the teacher with a simple unison action.

The children may like to imagine what they are angry about. Whatever the imagery, it is the resolving of the dance or phrase in *movement* terms which must be clear.

Summary

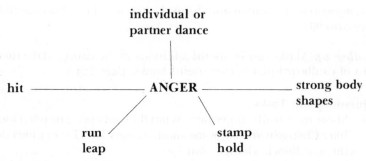

individual or
partner dance

hit ———————— ANGER ———————— strong body
shapes

run
leap

stamp
hold

Animals

208   CAT

stretch
leap
pounce
dash

Remember to repeat each phrase many times, and accompany it with voice or percussion.

Accompaniment voice sounds and words, a tape recording of a cat purring.

Follow up cat poems.

Questions and Tasks

1 What does a cat do? How does he move? (Select action words.)
2 Standing in your own space, stretch yourself into a curved shape. Arch backwards or curve over forwards.
3 Try kneeling. Stretch out into a curve. Try on all fours.
4 Now lie on the floor and curve yourself forwards and backwards quickly. Really move your back.
5 From your space, run and leap into the air. Stop suddenly. And again!
6 What shape did you make yourself in the air? What did you look like when you stopped?
7 Everyone practise this child's curved shape in the air. See how his arms stretch up and back.
8 All practise leaping and stopping many times.
9 With a partner, practise a pouncing jump down onto the floor. Move one after the other.
   First ones - Ready . . .
   Second ones - Ready . . .
Now altogether . . . dash and hide yourselves!

10   What do you look like when you stop? Are you really still?
11   Who can show me a pounce jump down towards the floor?
12   With a partner, practise pouncing. Move one after the other.
     First ones - ready . . .
     Second ones - ready . . .

The Dance
1   *A story framework*
    Cats stretch and stretch and jump up;
    leap high and pounce low upon their prey;
    run and hide themselves.
Each action is repeated rhythmically many times. The teacher's accompaniment helps make it dance-like. Then the children perform the dance in their own time (if they are ready for this) without the help of the teacher.
2   *A poem and voice accompaniment*
    The children make up a short, vocal, action poem, making the words sound like the action, using lots of repetition. Half the class dances as the other half says the poem.
3   *An individual dance*
    This could be based on the one work 'Pounce'. Make a pouncing dance to vigorous accompaniment.

Summary

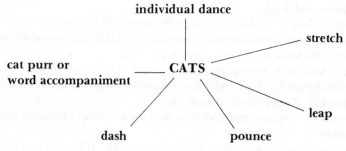

209 CROCODILE

wriggle
look
creep

This is a lesson for young children which might arise from poetry or story. Each movement is practised in short phrases, with clear going and stopping. The emphasis is on vivid movement sensation. Use the voice qualitatively.

Follow up a large, collage crocodile.

Questions and Tasks
1   Show me how the crocodile moves along. He wriggles along:
      Wriggle and wriggle and wriggle and *stop*.
2   Every time the crocodile *stops* he looks at me with his little red eye. And again:
      Wriggle and wriggle and look (at me).
3   This is a happy crocodile. He wriggles on his stomach and on his back.
    Can *you* wriggle on your shoulders?
4   Creep back to me fast like a hunter in the jungle.
5   Now the hunters *creep* through the jungle. They creep near the ground and high over the tree-trunks. They stop and listen. You show me your careful creeping:
      Creep and creep and creep and creep and *freeze*.
6   Sit by me.
    This is the wriggling sound (a tambourine shaking gently). This is the creeping sound (tapping the woodblock). (Move with fingers only.)
    Then who can creep with the creeping sound? (Choose some children.)
    Who can wriggle with the wriggling sound? (Choose some.)
7   Only those children find a space.
    When I play for wriggling, let's see if the wrigglers can wriggle. The creeping ones keep *still*.
    When I play for creeping, the creeping ones creep and the wriggling ones keep still.
    (This may have to be broken down still more.)

The Dance

The hunters and the crocodiles

Each group moving and stopping with its own sound accompaniment. At the end, perhaps the crocodiles go to sleep and the hunters creep back to the teacher.

Summary

dance in
two groups

wriggle
slither

**CROCODILE
STORY**

two contrasting
sounds

creep
look

210 DINOSAUR

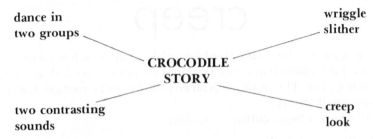

Enormous
rising, sinking
crawling,
slithering

Many different dances have evolved from these word actions. One class used the word 'ENORMOUS' as self-accompaniment to the movement (see Chants 121).

Follow-up work has included making a large dinosaur out of boxes stuck together, and dinosaur drawings which combine drawing and word patterns, i.e. making the name of the dinosaur into a design.

Questions and Tasks

1 Look at these pictures. What do they look like? Yes, huge, great, long creatures. They are very tall. Let's try making ourselves as tall and huge as possible.

2 Start near the ground. Now rise up very strongly and slowly. Get as big as you can and sink down to the ground again as though you were appearing out of the mud. Again. Listen to the sound of the tambour getting louder and louder as you get higher.

3 Can you make your hands go high as you rise up?

4 What other part of you could lead you high? Good. I can see chests going high, elbows, head.

5 Rise up and sink down now, three times. Make the movements flow together. (Yes, it is like coming out to have a look.) Make a sequence.

6 Try rising and sinking with your *partner*. Begin together. Show me two huge creatures rising and sinking.

7 How did the dinosaurs move along? Show me four huge crawls. Ready . . .
One, two, three and four and *still*.

8 Make the crawls much bigger. Stretch out the arms and the legs.

9 Which direction can you crawl in? Show me.

10 Good. Everyone try a *sideways* crawl. Now a turning one which stretches you right up and then down again.

11 Look at the shape of this dinosaur (picture). He is covered in spikes.

12 Can you make a huge, spiked shape and change it quickly to another one? . . . And again. Practise this.

13 As I point to you, crawl to me and make a spiky shape near me.

14 Let's try again. Can we make a long, spiky shape out of the whole class - a class dinosaur? Make the class dinosaur by moving, one by one, to make a central group.

The Dance

1 *A class dinosaur*
The children rise and sink strongly in place. At a given signal, one by one they crawl to the centre of the room, joining on their shape to the one already there so that a large, long, group shape is made. This can then travel and sink down to rest.
This idea could also be enacted in small groups.

2 *A partner dance*
Make a very short dance about dinosaurs. How do you begin? Do you move towards each other or around? How does it end?
These questions help *stimulate* invention or *clarify* what the children have made. Set a time limit for the invention.

Summary

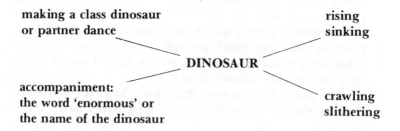

making a class dinosaur
or partner dance

rising
sinking

DINOSAUR

accompaniment:
the word 'enormous' or
the name of the dinosaur

crawling
slithering

211 DOG

shake
jump
listen

This lesson uses simple, whole-body action for young children, and encourages *where* they move in the space. Remember that small children love repetition and will enjoy repeating rhythmic phrases over and over again.

Questions and Tasks

1 Can you shake yourself all over like the dog when he's been in the water?
   Shake, shake, shake, shake, shake, shake.
2 This time, jump high in the air as you shake. Shake your *feet* in the air.
3 Now *run* and *stop,* into a new space.
4 Run and *stop* again. When you stop, *listen.* Wait for the next running sound. Which space are you going to run into next time? Here comes the sound . . .
5 Good. Now half of you sit near me. The other half spread along the wall. Lie on your side like dogs asleep.
   You're going to wake up
   Shake yourselves all over and
   Run into a space.

When you get there you are so happy to be let out you jump and jump on your space.

Ready and . . .

Shake and shake and run . . . and jump, jump, jump

Good *turning* jumps, feet *high in the air* jumps.

6 Now the next group lie down. Let's see *you* waking up. Wake up every bit of your body, your arms, head etc.

7 There was a good waking-up idea. Everyone lie on your *back* and stretch your legs high in the air.

And shake them hard . . . and jump to your feet

And again shake your legs and jump to your feet.

8 Everyone creep to me and sit.

The Dance

A with-the-teacher dance

Begin near the teacher. Jump up, shake yourselves, run into a space and jump and jump. When the teacher calls, creep back to her and sit down.

A whistling sound might be used by the teacher as a 'listen' signal.

Summary

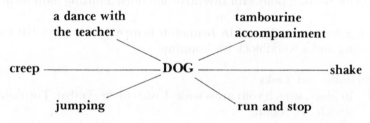

Nature

212 BIRDS

glide
shake
hop

Photographs of bird flight which show the different flying shapes help the idea, as does the observation of seagulls flying, converging, separating. Different types of birds—sparrows, eagles, penguins - can provide starting points for inventive and often amusing movement!

Suggested music 'Dawn' by Benjamin Britten, or use a cymbal for gliding and a woodblock for hopping.

Questions and Tasks

1 In place, stretch your arms wide. Listen to the cymbal. Turn and stretch . . . Again.
2 Dip down at your turn. Make one arm *glide* down, then the other. Bend and stretch as you glide up and down.
3 Now fly, glide stretched out wide to another space and glide up and down in that space.
4 Glide back to me and balance (hover).
5 *Shake* out your wings. Really vigorously, and again.
6 Shake and jump up and down - like a bird in a bird-bath. Shake one side and then the other side.
7 How does a bird *hop*? He hops and stops. Try hop and stop three times and then listen. Turn your head sharply.
8 Where do you hop? That was a good idea - two hops *forward* and then some turning hops.
9 Find some arm movements to fit the hopping.
10 Half the class sits in the centre of the room. The other half glides and swoops around and come to stillness and balance.

11 Half the class glides amongst the other half who stand preparing
    to hop. Then the gliding group balance still while the hopping
    ones move. Have two sounds - cymbal and woodblock - to
    accompany.

The Dance

1 *A gliding and swooping dance*
   Half the class glides and swoops and the other half balances.
   Change over smoothly.
2 *A sequence*
   Make a sequence of bird actions performed in groups or indivi-
   dually.

Summary

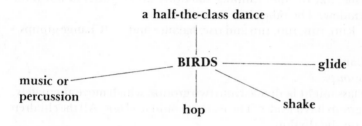

213 RAIN

beat
clap
run and rise

The excitement of this dance lies in the contrast between the strong,
vigorous movement *in place*, and the light, flowing, *travelling*
movement. The idea originally arose from watching rain beating
against the window. Action words were quickly selected from the
children's suggestions. The rhythm of the *lesson* was fast. Movement
preparation (e.g. rising before running) was stressed.

Follow up making 'Rain' poems.

Questions and Tasks

1   Everyone in his own space. Rise up on your toes and . . . BEAT down onto the floor, and again . . .

2   Try beating with your *feet* (accompany with quick tapping on a tambourine). And beating your *hands* on the floor. Beat your feet on the floor and then your hands.

3   Can you beat your feet, then jump in the air? And beat your hands and jump in the air? (Otherwise the movement stays at a low level.)

4   Where else can we beat our hands? Yes, on our bodies and *clapping* high above our heads. Try that. Ready . . .

5   You make your beating, clapping rain dance in the air, on the floor, on your bodies. Lots of movement . . .

6   Everyone sit. Now half of you are going to run smoothly, arms wide, like the rain running smoothly in the gutter or down the window. The other half sit still. Ready.

Run, run, run, run and *rise*, balance and . . . (Change groups.)

The Dance

Two groups

This class might be divided into two groups, which move alternately. Each group has a leader. The teacher could lead one. All the children move on the rhythm.

R-u-n and rise,

Beat on the floor, *beat* on the floor, *beat* on the floor, stop. The second group begins as the first group stops. This idea is repeated many times over.

So that one group is still while the other moves, but the rhythm is kept going. An exciting interplay develops.

Summary

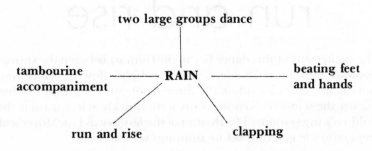

two large groups dance

tambourine accompaniment ——— RAIN ——— beating feet and hands

run and rise   clapping

stretch
curl
shoot out

This dance contrasts sustained and sudden movement and group versus individual activity.

Accompaniment percussion for the first part and quick, bright music for the second, such as Mendelssohn's Scherzo from music for 'Midsummer Night's Dream'.

Follow up a tissue-paper collage using 'hot colours'. Build up layers of tissue paper and glue for a 'sunset' effect. (See poem 'The Sun' included in **149**.)

Questions and Tasks

1   Look at the picture (or imagine) the sun rising. What can you see? The light coming out - the rays of the sun appearing.
2   Sit near me. Clench your fists near your chest. Now slowly uncurl, stretch your fingers, your hands, your arms and slowly curl in again. And again.
3   Now I'll play the cymbal and you practise that. Show me where your hands go in the space (some high, some sideways).
4   Stand, then curl near me. Slowly, starting with your fingers, uncurl and then stretch away from me. Stay there and slowly come back again. We are like the sun rising, getting bigger and bigger and sinking down again. Do that three times.
5   Shake yourself out really hard - your arms, your back, your legs. Run to a new space and shake yourself in your new space.
6   In your new space let's think now how the sun shoots out its beams all over the sky. Ready:
      Shoot your arms out and back again
      shoot your leg out and back again
      shoot one arm and one leg out and back again
      shoot everything out and back again.

7 Listen to the sound. Show me how you shoot out into the space. You choose what parts of you move. Perhaps it's going to be all of you.

8 Now *run* lightly, shooting your fingers and knees into the air as you go.

9 Stretch out wide like a huge sun and now slowly sink to the ground, down, down, like a sun setting.

The Dance

This can be enacted with the teacher, a partner or a small group.

Begin close to each other at a low level. Slowly stretch out so the group gets bigger and then shoot and dart into the space, leaving the group, sometimes travelling, sometimes on the spot. Return to the group and sink down slowly altogether.

Summary

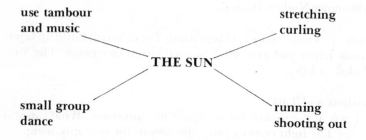

use tambour
and music

stretching
curling

THE SUN

small group
dance

running
shooting out

215 WATER

whirling
splashing up
rocking

'Whirl' and 'toss' are developed more fully than 'run' and 'rock'. Help the children *link* actions together. The use of real water produces vivid quality in the movement.

Questions and Tasks

1 Look at the water in the bowl. It's very still. Stretch your hands in front of you (palms down) and make your hands still like the surface of the water. Move them a little and then still again.

2 Watch what I make the water do. I'm making a whirlpool. Find a space. Show me a whirlpool movement. Ready . . . and stop very still.

3 Let's practise some of the ways you found . . . Turn on two feet, stretching out the arms wide.

4 Now whirl the arms upwards and downwards. Sometimes one arm, sometimes two. Make your whole body join in the movement.

5 Try whirling on your bottom. Can you keep your legs up? And then jump up and hop, whirl on one leg. And stop.

6 Turn very slowly, getting lower and lower until you are sitting.

7 Now watch the water. What is it doing? Splashing up and coming down.

8 Let's do that with our hands. Yes, it's a *sudden*, movement up into the air.

9 Standing, listen to the tambourine. Make sudden, splashing jumps into the air.

10 Now use hands or feet 'splashing' upwards.

11 Good, I saw one girl there toss her arms into the air, then turn and jump her knees into the air.

12 Listen to the sound. When I smooth and rub the tambourine, I want you to dance
   whirlpool
   When I shake and hit the tambourine change to
   tossing and leaping.

13 Come close to me now and sit down, not touching, so that you have space to move a little. Watch the water *rocking*.

14 Everyone rock like the water and then stop very still.

The Dance

1 *An individual dance*
   Begin near the teacher. Run and pause, run and pause in the free space of the hall. Choose your own space and whirl and toss there. Smoothly return to the teacher. slowly turn and sit rocking gently to stillness.

2 *A group dance*
   Use the above ideas. Each group chooses a particular action and moves in turn.

Summary

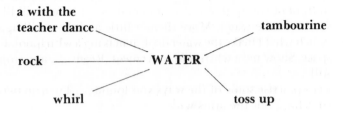

a with the
teacher dance

tambourine

rock ——————— WATER

whirl

toss up

216 WAVES

rising
sinking
rolling
pressing

Stress variations of these 'pair actions'. Give clear voice rhythms.
Stress movement flow. The movement could be linked to a story of a
tidal wave. A large piece of fabric might simulate a wave. Two children move it. The others rise and sink, copying the movement.

Accompaniment voice sounds or 'Surf' from BBC Sound Effects.

Questions and Tasks
1 Rise up high like the wave does, and then sink downwards and
   rise up again. Lead with your *hands.*
2 Try that group by group. Stretch really high. Lift your arms and
   legs.
3 See if you can fall bit by bit. Let your head go, your arms,
   shoulders, back, knees, so that your crumple downwards. Show
   me your falls, like waves breaking.

4 Group by group once again, rising, falling and rising. See if you can make a wave rhythm. Keep the movement going. Work on your *sequences.*

5 What do people do in the surf?
  Roll and press upwards to the surface again.

6 Imagine now the surf rolls you over. Ready.
  Roll and stop. And again. Roll in the surf.

7 I saw a roll and a kick upwards, a slow roll onto the knees with the arms floating up. Let's practise those ways.
  (Roll and kick, and roll and kick.)

8 Make it clear:
  How you rolled over
  How you press upwards to the surface again.
  (Pick out sequences. Encourage practising).

The Dance
A short dance of action and reaction arranged by the teacher. Either:
Half the class
  Rises and falls and rises like a huge wave
  Half the class rolls and presses upwards. Or:
A partner dance

Summary

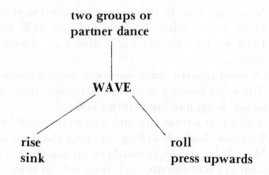

169

whirl
fall
leap
sway

The dance is about the movement of people in the wind.

Accompaniment try Debussy's 'Le vent d'ouest' from *Piano Preludes Book I* or make wind sounds.

Questions and Tasks

1 Imagine you're caught in a whirlwind. Try *whirling* and *stopping* very firmly. Do that three times, alternate sides. Each time, open the arms wide as you whirl.
2 Now leap wide in the air as if the wind were tossing you high. Make it clear what the arms and legs do in the air.
3 Let's see half the class at a time now, *linking whirling* with *leaping*.
   (A short practise, pick out some good sequences.)
4 The wind blows you over. Try *falling, rolling* and *leaping* up again. Keep moving continuously.
5 A group at a time: run and *leap* in the wind. And run and leap.
6 Everyone begin kneeling, *swaying* the arms from side to side. Make it bigger. Sway until you are standing. Swing in the wind with big movements, rock from side to side.

The Dance

In four groups

Each group decides on one of the phrases of movement. They sort out starting positions and relationships towards and away from each other, one after the other etc. and perform one group after another, keeping a flow from group to group.

Summary

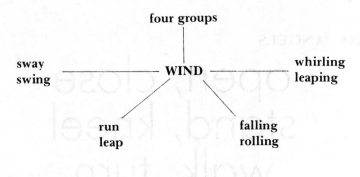

four groups

sway
swing

WIND

whirling
leaping

run
leap

falling
rolling

171

218 ANGELS

open, close
stand, kneel
walk, turn

Here the actions selected are very simple and the creativity lies in the making of simple sequences. Children quickly respond to the idea of linking actions together. It is particularly important to stress the full enactment of each action, such as the sensation of growing and stretching in the 'opening' action.

Accompaniment a slow-pace carol or Indian bells.

Questions and Tasks
1   What do angels look like? They have their *arms stretched* out open wide; sometimes they're standing, sometimes kneeling.
2   Move your arms slowly to the sound of the Indian bell. Gently open and close them.
3   Now kneel down slowly as you close them and *stand* slowly as you open them.
4   Try a *slow turn* with your arms stretching out wide. And the other way.
5   Perhaps you could *turn and kneel* and then stand slowly again.
6   Now *walk* forwards very smoothly opening your arms wide and then closing them again gently.
7   Choose which direction you do your angel walks in.
8   Now sometimes kneel, sometimes stand, sometimes walk, sometimes turn. Show me how *you* begin.
9   Make it clear what your arms do as you move. Are they *closing*? Are they *opening*?
10   Find a partner. See if you can work out some angel movement together. Are you both going to do the same movement or are you going to be different?

The Dance

1 *A group dance*

One by one, the children leave the group and reform in another space. This could involve standing, walking, opening, kneeling. Then the whole group moves together in some simple unison sequence.

2 *A partner dance*

A kneeling, standing angel; a turning, walking angel. Partners change over. Partners finish in a unison action.

3 *A file dance*

A simple follow-my-leader pathway and action, concluding with each angel leaving the file and settling gently in his/her own space.

Summary

a slow carol
or
Indian bells   opening and
                                closing arms

               ANGELS

walking   standing
turning   kneeling

219 FIREWORKS

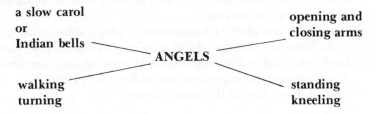

It is important to stress 'preparation and recovery', namely how the movement begins and how it ends. Repeat a phrase of movement many times - movement involvement grows with rhythmic repetition. The words could equally well be linked with other images, such as space craft which rocket up and disintegrate downwards. Have a brief discussion of fireworks, linking images to movement words.

Accompaniment voice sounds or 'Troyte' from Enigma Variations by Elgar.

Questions and Tasks

1 Everyone jump, shoot your whole self into the air. Lead the movement with the hands. Ready . . .
    Shoot into the air, and . . .

2 Try now: shoot into the air, land and come down slowly, drift down. Ready . . .
    Into the air and . . . softly down, down, down. Good, the arms were opening as you moved downwards.

3 What other parts could you shoot upwards? Your head, your knee? This time, vary the part that goes into the air. (Observe and encourage.)

4 Altogether now, try:
    Run and *knee* jump into the air (many times). Pull the knees right up as you jump.

5 In your new space, practise your sequence of *shoot up* and *drift down*. I'll give you three minutes. I'm going to walk round and see what you are making.

6 Good. (To one child) I liked that low preparation, arms well back. Then you shot into the air with your hands and knee high, landed and did a slow, spiral turn. Do that again many times. Try to control the movement and make it very clear.

7 And sit. How should this dance begin?

The Dance

The movement begins from one end of the hall, spreading from one child to the next (like fireworks being let off gradually) until the space is filled with shooting, drifting-down figures. Try a unison ending with everyone making large circles (catherine wheels) with their arms, gradually slowing down to stillness.

Voice sound accompaniment
Half the class accompanies, half moves. For example, use the sound:
s h sh sh sh T m m m m m m m m (humming)

Summary

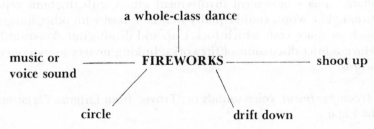

freeze
shatter
melt

This idea has been used with many different age groups. Adjust the imagery to suit the children. Use it in connection with looking at ice shapes in winter, or experiments with freezing water.

Accompaniment quiet chime bars or Indian bells.

Questions and Tasks

1   Icicles? . . . As I point to you, move very slowly into a space and grow into any icicle position. There can be all different shapes. Then melt a little and form a new shape. Keep moving slowly.

2   And come back to me. You had some very good ideas, but let's make them a little clearer. How could you make it better? Yes, you could make the icicles harder, stronger. Show me an icicle *hand,* an icicle *elbow.*

3   Now try the idea (no.1) again. Remember you can balance on different parts of yourself to make the icicle shape . . .

4   Hold the ice shape now. Imagine I throw a stone and break up the ice, *shatter* the ice. Ready and I THROW . . . Good, that made you really move. What did you *do?*

5   (Answers)
   You shot your hands into the air?
   You rolled and balanced?
   You kicked your toes upward?
   Let's see some of these. Make it clear what happens to you in movement; what you look like when you stop . . .

6   Everyone try again now. All the movements are sharp and sudden. Try several sharp movements in a row. Ready . . .
   And *move* and *move* and *move* (fast pace).

7   Now all of you do sharp skips around the room like sharp ice shooting into the air. Use shooting fingers too.
   Skip and skip and skip and skip and skip and *balance.* Is your knee sharp, your foot pointed?

8   And melt to the ground . . .
      Melt, melt, melt down into a puddle.
    And lie very relaxed.

The Dance
Two or three of these ideas could be drawn together in a subsequent
lesson; for example:
    the ice forms (individuals or groups of three)
    the ice breaks and scatters
    it melts.

Voice sounds
humming
sharp sounds (*ch, ch, st*)
could be used by the children as they dance.

Summary

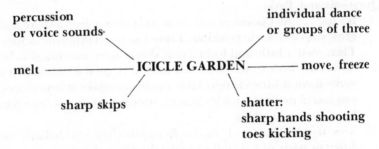

percussion
or voice sounds·

individual dance
or groups of three

melt ————————— ICICLE GARDEN ——————— move, freeze

sharp skips

shatter:
sharp hands shooting
toes kicking

221 STARS

star shapes
bouncing
shooting
disappearing

Make a simple silver star. Use it as a visual stimulus for body shape and movement. This is very useful where there are language problems.

Accompaniment triangle, tambourine.

Questions and Tasks

1 Sit near me. Look at the star. Can you make your hand look like that? And the other hand. Now hold up two star hands.

2 Make a star with two hands. Perhaps put your wrists or fingers together. Good. Every time I make a sound on the triangle, you make me star hands . . .

3 Who can bounce away from me into a *space* and make a *big* star there out of your whole body? Ready . . .

4 Good. Look at those stars. There are some on their knees and some balancing on one leg and . . . (feed in these ideas if necessary).

5 Now lots of times. Keep the movement going.
   Bounce and bounce and bounce and a STAR . . . (body shape).

6 Show me your last star shape. Now make your star disappear slowly into the ground. Down, down until you're lying down, limp and still. The stars have gone.

7 And come to crouch position. Now, suddenly there are some *shooting* stars. Ready, jump straight up and shoot your fingers in the air. Do that three times. And . . .
   Shoot and shoot and shoot.

8 *Run* and shoot, and
   Run and shoot and *balance*.
   Who can balance?
   And come to me.

The Dance

A few of these ideas could be drawn together. Suggest simply: 'Now you make me a star dance. I wonder how you are going to begin.'

Older children have made star dances 'mirroring' star shapes - moving slowly from lying to kneeling, standing, turning etc.

Summary

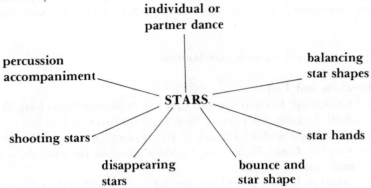

individual or
partner dance

percussion
accompaniment

balancing
star shapes

STARS

shooting stars

star hands

disappearing
stars

bounce and
star shape

Shapes and Sculpture

222 OVER, UNDER, AROUND

stepping
lifting
crawling
ducking

These words stimulate different ways of *travelling* along and group
shapes which are made by the children fitting in over, under and
around each other. The words are related to the image of a CAVE.

Questions and Task
1 Imagine we are in a cave. There are rocks in the way. You have to
get *over* the rocks. When the tambour rhythm stops, you pause so
I can see what you look like in the cave.
2 Good. I saw:
stepping over with the *knees* high
lifting the hands over, then the feet jumping over
Practise:
step over and over and rise
and
lift and *jump* and lift and *jump*.
3 Now in the same way, go *under* rocks. Yes,
ducking under
rolling under
sliding under
backbending under.
Make each movement big and clear.
4 Choose now going:
over, under and *around*.
Explore the cave.

5   See if we can make a rock shape out of bodies. In groups of three. Fit yourselves in close together so one is under, one is over the other. Make different-shaped rock groups. Practise moving slowly into one group shape and then slowly changing it into another.

The Dance
Half-the-class dance
Half the children makes rock shapes. The other half moves around the groups, and moves over and under imaginary rocks and, possibly, the 'rock children'.

Summary

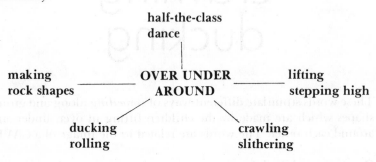

Sound

223 BOUNCE and SPIN

bounce, spin

A beginning lesson for young children stressing high and low, moving and stopping. Note that spin is not developed as much as bounce.

Accompaniment BBC Radiophonic 'Milky Way', and percussion.
Follow up a bounce, spin finger *painting*.

Questions and Tasks

1 Sitting, listen to this bouncy sound on my tambourine
    Bounce and *bounce* and *bounce*.
2 When the bouncy sound starts I want you to bounce your *fingers* on your knees, and when it stops, *you* stop and be very still. Ready . . . (several times).
3 This time I want you to listen to me as well as the bouncy sound, and I will call out which bit of you your hands must bounce on. Like this:
    Bounce your fingers on your knees.
4 As I *point to you* bounce away into a space and sit.
5 Show me your bounces in your space. Here's the bouncing sound . . .
6 Good. I saw some *high*, high ones and some *low* down ones. Show me now when you bounce high and when you bounce low.
7 Good, some children were opening their arms wide and then closing themselves up tight as they bounced.
8 All sit. Can you put your feet and legs in the *air* in front of you? Stretch them up and bring them down . . . Now who can *spin* on their bottoms with their legs off the ground? Ready, spin . . . Yes, you have to be very strong.
9 Now, stand and look around for another space. Point to that space. And this time:
    Bounce and bounce and bounce and BURST in that new space Ready . . .
    Who can stop very still? Are you all in terrible burst positions? Look how he's landed! And again:
    Bounce and bounce and bounce and BURST.

The Dance
An individual dance
A 'bounce and burst' dance, which is just a repetition of no.9, with the added directive of: 'Show me how you begin and how you end. I wonder what sort of bounce *you* are going to do.' Use music. Fade it for the last 'burst'.

Summary

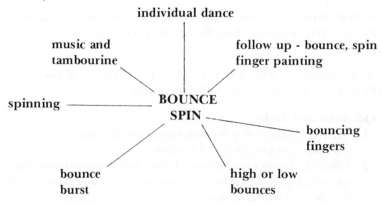

224   DRUM BEAT

Contrast *feet* movement with *shoulder* and *hand* or *fist* movement. Encourage older children to produce a definite *step pattern* through putting together steps, jumps, hops with the music.

Accompaniment 'Bang on a Drum', a Play Away song from BBC cassette MRMC 004, or 'Modern Primitive Beginners' Gamba Educational Records DCG 001

Questions and Tasks

1 What can your *feet* do to the music? Jumps? Show me.

2 Everyone try this one:
 Stamp, stamp, step - hop
 Stamp, stamp, step - hop.

3 Or *jump* the feet:
 across and apart
 across and apart
 or side to side
 forwards and backwards.

4 Try that sideways jump. Feet together. And:
 Bounce and bounce and a run-run jump.
 Make it go with the music.

5 Make *groups of three*. See if you can work out together a jumping, stepping pattern of movement. I will go round and help you.

6 Now make some *shoulder* movements, shrugging, or fist-beating movements:
 Shrug and a shrug and a beat, beat, beat. Make the movements large. Make the whole body join in.

7 Stand well spaced out, facing each other in threes. You are going to dance *one* at a time. The *first* one dances around the other *two* and back to place, and so on. The two who are not dancing around can use shoulder or fist movement on the spot.

The Dance

In threes

Each group works out a stepping, jumping pattern and decides *where* they shall move in relationship to each other. (Forwards and away, in and out etc.). The dance might end with groups meeting and mingling in the centre of the room.

 Younger children enjoy making freer variations of stepping, jumping, stamping, hopping with perhaps a simple *unison* step near the teacher to begin and end the dance.

Follow up making drum-beat rhythms; beating out *their* movement pattern; combining their 'tune' with another's; tape recording the rhythms.

Summary

follow up
making drum rhythms

|

music
accompaniment ——————DRUM BEAT —————— stepping,
jumping feet

/ \

dancing
in threes

shrugging shoulders
beating fists

225 FEET

Include a chant from *The Foot Book* by Dr Seuss (Collins and Harvill).

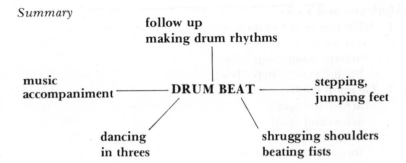

jump, hop
stride, shake
kick, turn

Dances based on *feet* can lead to a wide variety of styles and moods. They can be dramatic, or highly rhythmic.

Follow up (for young children) drawing different kinds of feet and then dancing the ideas.

Questions and Tasks

1 Shake your feet. Stamp your feet. Jump your feet. Run your feet and stop.
2 Here's a jumping rhythm (or sound). Show me jumping and stopping.
3 Jump your feet apart and then together. Really stretch them in the air.
4 Turn as you jump.
5 Stride on this fast rhythm to another space.
6 Practise hopping on one foot, then the other. What does the leg in the air do?

7   Sit down and *shoot both feet* up in the air. Curl your legs down
    and shoot your feet up again.
8   Can you make up some jumping, hopping feet movement?
    Here's a rhythm to help you.
9   All copy that big jump and three small hops. Keep it going. Feel
    the rhythm. Let's choose another one.
10 Let's use the foot chant for striding and jumping. Say it and do it
    with me:
        left foot right foot - (striding)
        left foot right foot - (striding)
        feet feet feet. - (jumping).

The Dance

1   *Individual choice* of movement with the wood block as accomp-
    animent, alternating with a class *unison action* using the chant as
    the accompaniment: dancing in your own space around the
    teacher; moving towards her on the chant.
2   *Very young children* enjoy the rhythmic enactment of simple
    action words:
        'my striding feet'
        'my jumping feet' etc.
3   *Older children* like making jumping, turning, skipping sequen-
    ces which can be as complex as their skills allow. Use fast-pace
    rhythmic music.

Summary

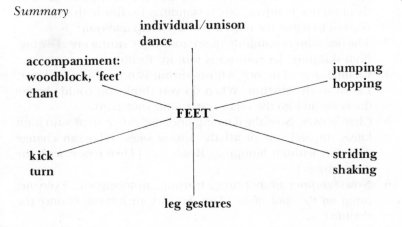

clap
skip
gallop
jump

The rhyme provides a vigorous rhythm for going and stopping actions. Changes of direction, added actions, and coordination of other body parts can be developed according to the age and ability of the children. The rhyme can also be a useful starting activity.

Questions and Tasks

1   Clap the rhythm with me. Stop when I stop. This half of the class clap when I point to *you*, and this half clap when I point to *you*. Don't get caught out - I might ask you twice running.

2   The first half of the class sit in a space. The second half stand by them (so one is sitting, one is standing. Do this with a running rhythm to make the movement very crisp and quick.)

3   The one who is standing, dance round the sitting one. Use big, high skipping, let your arms join in. Ready . . .

4   Change over. The one who is sitting is now going to dance. Listen to the rhythm. When do you think you could change direction and go the other way round your partner?

5   Change over. Now the dancing ones use *gallop* steps with high knees, in and out of all the sitting ones. Who can change direction without bumping? Ready . . . (Then repeat with the other group.)

6   Now *jumping* or hopping, turning, tiptoeing etc. Everyone jump on the spot or in place. See if your feet can bounce the rhythm.

7   What jumps are they? Good. I saw:
     Bounce, bounce, and land feet apart, and
     Hop, hop, jump them together, and
     Bounce, bounce, knees up jump.

8 Make a dance with your partner. I will give you two minutes. Use skipping, galloping or jumping. Make it clear what your arms do.

The Dance
A partner dance
After very directed tasks which improve the actions and serve as examples of relationships, the children freely explore the ideas within a partner relationship. The teacher helps them clarify the action and the relationship - towards and away, around and so on.

A simpler idea with very young children would be to have a galloping group, a jumping group and a skipping group, using the last rhythm for creeping back to the teacher.

Loud and quiet rhythms could be another development for changing from large to small movement.

Summary

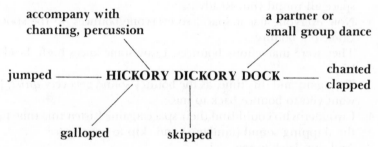

227 MAGIC SOUND

bounce
skip
clap

This is for a class of young children with very little movement experience. Stress body awareness and 'space words'; 'away from', 'back to', 'high'. The aim is to communicate some basic ways of moving and stimulate an interest in different ways of moving.

Accompaniment use a tambourine to begin with, then music, for example *American Dances* (EP 538).

Follow up look at pictures of animals or moving things. What do they do? Do the movements with arms and hands as they sit. Make collections of movement pictures.

Questions and Tasks

1 All sit near me and bounce your fists on the floor just as though your fists were like rubber balls:
   Bounce and bounce and bounce and bounce and stop. And higher bounces . . .
2 Now, one by one as I call your name, run and find *your* space on the floor and sit there. It mustn't be near a wall. You must have a space all round you. Ready . . .
3 Now everyone has a space, so everyone bounces on the spot. Come on, bounce . . .
   They were marvellous bounces. I saw some knees high, heads high.
   Try again and this time, as the bouncy sound gets very *quiet*, I want you to bounce back to me.
4 I wonder who could find their space again? Listen this time to the skipping sound (tambour) and skip to your space . . .
   And skip back to me.
5 Sit near me and listen to the music. You all sit like statues. When the music begins, you come alive and clap and bounce your hands to the music. Good, clapping high and clapping low.
6 Let's make a dance now. Stand like statues near me. When the music begins it brings you alive. You *skip* away to your own space, then make a *bouncing, clapping* dance on your own space. As the music gets quieter, you skip back to me and turn into a statue again.

The Dance
With the teacher
Many infant dances can follow this plan: starting near, travelling into the space and returning.
   Different actions could obviously be used.

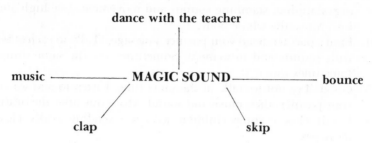

228 MESSAGES WITH SOUND

clicking
stamping
slapping

Experiment with making sounds through clicking the fingers, stamping the floor, slapping the body etc. Make sequences of sounds. These are the messages Indians used to send. Develop high and low so the body is fully involved.

Accompaniment music could be used - perhaps an extract from Rimsky-Korsakov 'Capriccio Espagnol'.

Questions and Tasks

1 Everyone listen hard. I am going to send you a *message* with my feet. You send the same message back:
   (teacher) Stamp, stamp - stamp - stamp
   (children) Stamp, stamp - stamp - stamp.
2 Try some more sounds now (fast pace, lots of examples). *Clicking* fingers high and low and all around the body:
   clapping and leaping
   stamping forwards and backwards
   slapping rhythms on the body:
   slap the side, the feet, the hands
   slap the side, the feet, the hands.

3   Everyone now make up your own message. You can make click-
    ing, slapping, stamping sounds and movement. Use high and
    low. Move the whole body.

4   Find a partner. Send your partner a mesage. 'Talk' to each other
    with sounds and movement. Sometimes say the same thing,
    sometimes different.

5   Good. Try not to 'talk' at the same time. Listen to and watch
    your partner, then move and sound. Move one after the other.

6   I will choose some children who are sending really clear
    messages.

The Dance
A partner dance using contrasting sequences of body-part action.
The expression may become witty or angry. Encourage copying the
message or sending back a *different* one.

Summary

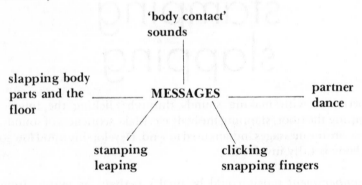

'body contact'
sounds

slapping body
parts and the _____ MESSAGES _____ partner
floor   dance

stamping   clicking
leaping   snapping fingers

229 NAMES

stepping
turning
bouncing
circling

Aim for variety of movement through moving to the *rhythm* of the child's name. Give several examples and encourage full enactment of the movement to the rhythm. Action to a specific rhythm needs to be repeated many times.

Questions and Tasks

1   Sit near me. All say and clap Angela's name together:
    Angela Viber, Angela Viber
2   Everyone in a space. Ready, say and move the name:
    Angela Viber *Ange*la Viber
    Stepping and *Jump*ing
    Stepping and *Jump*ing.
    Try it lots of times. Make it clear when you step, when you jump.
3   Good, look at those *arms* - they swing across and *open* to accent the jump. Everyone show me four times now with the rhythm . . .
4   Now, quickly form a circle. I'll point to someone. We'll all say her name. Lots of times. Then we'll say it and dance it. You can jump it, stamp it, turn it. Use high and low. Keep on saying and moving. Keep it going. Ready . . .
    Harpreet *Gup*ta, Harpreet *Gup*ta
5   Good, let's all do turning and stamping. That turn with the arms stretched out:
    Harpreet Gupta . . .
    Turn and stamp stamp . . .
6   Now a faster travelling one. Use it for bouncing and hopping to another space.
    Derek Joseph, Derek Joseph
    and *stop*.
7   Everyone sit near me. Let's all say:
    Sangeeta Ahluwalia
    a beautiful *long* name. Make big smooth circles with arms and head. Ready . . .

The Dance

Many ideas might evolve, including, perhaps, and individual leading to a unison dance.

1   The children begin moving, whispering and dancing their own name. Stress body parts. The sound increases, the movement gets larger.
2   A sudden stop.
3   They all dance around one child, chanting his name.
    (Think of an ending.)

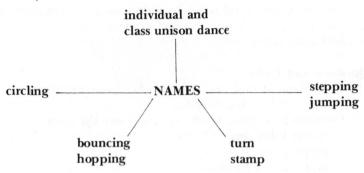

individual and
class unison dance

circling ———— NAMES ———— stepping
jumping

bouncing
hopping

turn
stamp

230 PERCUSSION DANCE

(Use shakers made from small, decorated containers filled with rice,
peas etc.)

shaking
hitting

The instrument is used to encourage moving high and low and
around with a partner. Younger children can play alone or with the
teacher. For preference use home-made shakers, small enough to
handle easily. Preparatory classroom work in picking up, putting
down, shaking it and holding it still, is useful.

Questions and Tasks

1   Half the class sit near me. The other half find a space and stand
    with your shakers stretched high above your head.
2   Now *shake* it and hit it high and low. Ready . . . Three times . . .
    You must really *stretch* as high as you can and *bend* your knees
    to play it low. (Change over groups.)
3   This group play it so high in the air that you have to jump or
    skip . . . Play it on the spot. (Change over group.)
4   This group do eight skips to another space as you play the
    shaker. Start *low*, end high on your toes. Ready . . . And one and
    two and three (etc.) And again. This time *turn* as you play . . .
    (Change groups.)

5　Everyone in a space. Reach out with your shaker *far* from your body. Now play it around the body in big circles. Yes, over your head and round, and up high and behind you.
Really stretch your body into the space.

6　Try changing over hands as you play. Hold the shaker in one hand, then the other.

The Dance
A partner dance
Make a shaker dance together. Do you stay on the same spot or do you travel around your partner with the shaker? Use high and low.

Summary

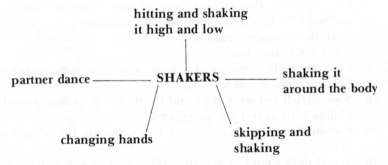

231　SAUSAGES, CHIPS and ICE-CREAM

Choose from the children's favourite foods or drinks to make 'food rhythms'. Note the repetition to evolve movement rhythms. Use contrasting movement to express the words. Experiment with different ways of *'saying'* and different ways of *moving*.

Follow up tape record a chant, or play the rhythm on percussion instruments.

Questions and Tasks

1   What's your favourite food? Sausages, chips and ice-cream. How should we say 'sausages'? Slowly and softly.

2   Move your arms softly and slowly, twisting and turning them gently up and down. Say 'sausages' gently as you move.

3   Now move your backs, bending and stretching, moving up and down. Use your shoulders too.

4   Say 'chips' very sharply. As you say 'chips', shoot up into the air. Repeat the word 'chips'. Show me your jump to 'chips'.

5   I saw a shooting jump with the feet together followed by a hop, then a turning jump. Let's all try that:
       chips, chips, chips
       jump, hop and turning jump.

6   Find a partner. One say and move 'sausages', then the other say and move 'chips'. Think of a starting position.
       All the 'sausages', ready . . .
       All the 'chips', ready . . .

7   Everyone gather near me. Let's say 'ice-cream' very smoothly. Repeat it lots of times.

8   Now stretch out your arms and hands and do a big, smooth, gliding turn as you say 'ice-cream'.

9   Say and move 'ice-cream' several times. Do you finish high or low?

10 Try gliding round now with another part of you leading the movement. Perhaps your elbows or one foot. Keep it very smooth.

11 Now choose whether you like sausages, chips or ice-cream movement best. When I hold up the word 'sausages', only the 'sausage' people move. Keep on repeating the word. Show me your movement ideas. Repeat with 'chips' and 'ice-cream'.

12 Now all say and do your food at the same time.

The Dance

A dance near the teacher - everyone chanting quietly, 'sausages, chips and ice-cream'. At a signal from the teacher they whisper their way to their own space. The children have already decided who is going to say 'sausages', who 'chips', who 'ice-cream'. They choose a starting position which could relate to the shape of the food they are chanting. All the 'sausages' say and move, perhaps four times, and freeze; then the 'chips' move and then the 'ice-cream'. To end, all simultaneously say their food loudly, becoming softer, and finish on the floor. (This would suit young children.)

Older children could work in twos or threes, sharing the words and the movement between them. Questions such as, 'Do you move at the same time or one after the other?' help clarify the ideas.

Summary

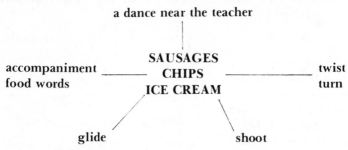

Poetry

232 FOG

This poem by Carl Sandburg comes from *Wordscapes* by Barry Maybury (Oxford University Press).

Fog
The fog comes
on little cat feet,
It sits looking
over harbour and city
on silent haunches
and then moves on.

spreading
tiptoeing
swirling

The poem is a starting image for ideas arising from 'Fog'. The main quality in the lesson is lightness. Therefore, have a vigorous warm-up. Note the movement contrasts. Make sure that the body is fully extended. Give rhythms, especially in (no. 3), for practising the movements.

Accompaniment use the action words to encourage qualitative movement. Later, add background music from BBC Radiophonic.

Questions and Tasks
1 Close your eyes while I read the poem. Can you see the picture in your mind? What does it look like (etc.)? 'It's very white and soft,' says one child. 'It moves slowly.'
2 Sit by me and put your fingers together very gently, hardly touching. Now move them apart into the space as if you are making the fog, spreading the fog all around you with your hands and fingers (very gently opening and closing the arms).

3   Can you tiptoe 'in little cat feet' into a space of your own? . . .
     Now stretch up and out on tiptoe. Then make the fog all around
     you with your fingertips. Make it high, make it to the side (etc.)
4   Stretch up high and wide . . .
     Tiptoe into another space and make the fog in the new space.
5   Now half of you are going to be quite still in your space
     anywhere on the floor. You choose whether you are kneeling, or
     curled on your side, or stretching high . . .
6   The other half spread out in the spaces between them . . . You are
     going to move amongst them, spreading fog.
     This time the fog moves *fast, swirling* and stretching and
     changing direction . . . Then listen to the cymbal. Slow down and
     stop with the sound.
7   There were some lovely movements there. Some people were
     really stretching high and opening their arms far away from
     their bodies, and then closing down really low.
8   Change places and let's see if the second group can listen to the
     cymbal as it makes you go faster and slower.
     The ones who aren't spreading fog? . . . Yes, you could be like
     people moving very slowly in the fog. Can you try moving
     slowly from standing, to kneeling, to sitting as the fog swirls
     around you? Ready . . .
9   Can everyone practise that *swirling turn?* Look how he starts
     with his arms stretched high and then dips them down to one
     side, turns and opens them high. Everyone try . . .
10   How shall we make our fog dance?

The Dance

The fog comes from everywhere. The children crouch at the sides of
the room. They gradually move - first of all tiptoeing, then swirling
with faster and larger movements. As the cymbal stops, they freeze
their position. The teacher moves amongst them, touching them
gently, and they gently sink to a lying position. The fog has gone.

Summary

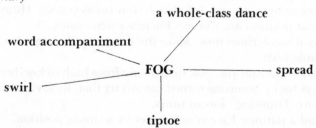

233   HUMBUG

from the poem, *Bug Words*
(to be said when grumpy)

> HUMBUG
> BUGBEAR
> BUGABOO
> BUGBANE
> LADYBUG
> BODYBUG
> BUGSEED

Alastair Reid from *Junior Voices, Book 3*

grip
swing
stamp - leap

The action words chosen are arbitrary. Relate the words to *body-part* movement. 'Humbug' is a strong, angry word which goes with strong, angry movement sequences. Say it fast, say it slowly. (See Body part contrasts **16**.)

Questions and Tasks

1   All sit by me. Say 'Humbug' with me loudly and clearly. Ready .. And again . . .

2   As you say it, *grip* your fists tightly. Ready . . . 'Humbug!' Now say it inside your head, but still make the movement *strong*.

3   Find yourself a space on the floor and take up any strong position, standing - fists clenched - legs strong.

4   Now swing your arm and clench your fist as you say 'Humbug!' What position are you in? There's a fierce one.

5   Say it many times now. Make the swings really large. Use your whole body.

6   Good, some people took their swing from high to low, bending their backs. Someone turned his. All try that. Ready . . . Say and move 'Humbug!' lots of times.

7   Find a partner. Face your partner in a strong position.

8 This time, open wide and then do an *enormous leap* as you say:
    'Humbug!'
   Both together - Ready:
    'Humbug!'
   Use your arms and your legs as you leap.
9 Now move one after the other. Really high. Really strong. Finish
   high or low.
10 Make your dance with your partner. Move and say 'Humbug'.
   Make it fierce with big movements. Show me how you begin -
   how you end. Use sequences of movement. Find some more big,
   strong movements and body shapes.
11 Good. Two boys here are using:
    Open and leap, swing and fists.
   They are using the *same* movement. Another two are:
    Swinging down into a *roll* and a leap
    Leaping using fists.
   That was a new idea.
12 Everyone quite still. Show me you dance . . . Finish quite still.
13 Everyone quietly back to me. Listen to these words:
    HUMBUG, BUGBANE, LADYBUG, BODYBUG,
    BUGSEED.
14 All say them . . .
   All whisper them . . .
   Now each of you *choose* one.
   Now all say your word *loudly* at the same time.
   Ready . . .

The Dance
1 A partner dance based on one word.
2 A partner dance based on two words.
3 A class dance - everyone sounds and moves his word one by one.
   Then all sound together many times, moving vigorously. At a
   signal, they *whisper* their word and return to a sitting position.
The next lesson could develop this content into a richer assortment of
strong movement, or more *practice* of observed actions.

   Other words, angrily spoken, could be alternative accompaniment - names of things they dislike, perhaps.

Summary

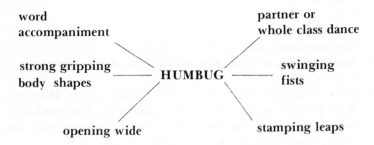

word
accompaniment

partner or
whole class dance

strong gripping
body shapes ——— **HUMBUG** ——— swinging
fists

opening wide

stamping leaps

234 'THE RAIN DANCE'

The Rain Dance
The fire flickered with a flare,
The ghostly figure *leapt in the air.*
Huge shadows fell across the ground
When the figure landed without any sound.
A piercing scream, a bongo beat,
A tossing head, two stamping feet.
Legs bent at knees, feet wide apart,
A twisting body, a thudding heart.
The drums beat out, loud and clear.
D-rr-um-dum-dum, the time draws near.
The twirling body leaps again
Trying hard to make it rain.

Marina Brunskill from *Wordscapes* by Barry Maybury (Oxford
University Press).

Use these words as a basis for action phrases. Some children could
clap and chant the words while others dance. Emphasize the *landing*
in the jump.

leap, land
toss, stamp

Questions and Tasks

1 Stand still and straight. Bounce very gently. Feel the floor with your feet, very easy, no sound on landing. And still. Remember it's all very quiet.

2 Now I want you to do a *large* jump on the spot and land *very* gently. It's like a cat jump - very careful. Ready and . . . JUMP!

3 Good. Can you see how it makes the ending of your jump - your position - very important? Now try a jump from two feet landing on one. Ready, with the rhythm, four of those jumps and soft, soft landings . . .
Anywhere round the room, huge jumps and *soft* landings.

4 Everyone join in as I say the words:
The fire flickered with a flare,
The ghostly figure leapt in the air.
Huge shadows fell across the ground
When the figure landed without any sound.

5 Half of you sit in a circle - you are going to chant and clap.
Half of you stand inside the circle - you are going to practise:
Leap and land.
This is in the darkness around a fire. I'll beat the drum too.
The centre group practise:
leap and land
as the circle claps and chants. Ready. Come on now, up on your toes, open your arms, prepare to leap and . . . (chant).

6 Change over groups.

7 Try the same idea with 'toss and stamp'. Chant and clap:
A tossing head, two stamping feet.

8 Everyone stand and move to the words. You must toss your head high, bend your knees and make the stamps sharp. They don't have to be hard. I'll play the rhythm on the drum. You fit your tossing and stamping into the drum beat. Ready . . .

The Dance

A *circle dance* with an inner and outer group contrasting activities:
Quiet clapping from the circle.
Inner group begin (one after another) leaping and landing until they are all leaping.
A sudden stop.
Inner group sit and begin clapping the toss, stamp rhythm.
The outer group circle around them tossing and stamping.
Devise an ending. Perhaps everyone sinks down, spread-eagled on the ground, waiting for the rain.

Summary

a half-the-class
dance

accompaniment
words, drumbeat

RAIN DANCE

toss
stamp

leap
land

235 'THE WANDERING MOON'

The Wandering Moon
Age after age and all alone.
  She turns through endless space,
Showing the watchers on the earth
  Her round and rocky face.
Enchantment comes upon all hearts
  That feel her lonely grace.

Mount Newton is the highest peak
  Upon the wandering moon,
And there perhaps the witches dance
  To some fantastic tune,
And in the half-light cold and grey
  Their incantations croon.

And there perhaps mad creatures come
  To play at hide-and-seek
With howling apes and blundering bears
  And bats that swoop and squeak.
I cannot see what nameless things
  Go on at Newton Peak.

I cannot tell what vessels move
  Across the Nubian Sea,
Not whether any bird alights
  On any stony tree.
A quarter of a million miles
  Divide the moon and me.

A quarter of a million miles -
  It is a fearsome way,
But ah! if we could only fly
  On some auspicious day
And land at last on Newton Peak,
  And then, what games we'd play!

What songs we'd sing on Newton Peak,
  On what wild journeys go
By frozen fen or burning waste,
  Or where the moon-flowers grow,
And countless strange and fearful things -
  If only we could know!

James Reeves from *Complete Poems for Children* (Heinemann).

turn, circle
run, stop
twist
grow, shrivel

Introduce the poem before the dance lesson. Choose one image from each verse.

Accompaniment background percussion sounds. Children could make up the accompaniment.

Questions and Tasks

1   Think of the shape of the moon. Draw a huge, moon-shaped circle in front of the body with your right arm.
    Stretch high over to the side, down to the floor and back. Bend and stretch your legs.
2   Try stretching and circling one arm, then the other and *turn* slowly and smoothly.

3 All sit by me. Remember that we decided that the 'mad creatures' move fast and stop in weird shapes. (Still sitting) - first of all practise moving your *hands* fast in every direction. Move the hands:

    suddenly high

    suddenly sideways (etc.)

4 Find a space. Listen to the woodblock. Practise short runs and stops in:

    mad shapes.

Use different directions.

5 There's a good one. He stopped with his head near the ground, hand and one heel in the air. Everyone practise, run and stop, with a part of you high in the air.

The Dance

The words: twisting (witches) and strange growing (moonflowers) could be similarly explored. Make a dance in

four groups based on:

    moon

    witch

    mad creatures

    moonflower

each with a different percussion accompaniment.

One class devised a unison ending to the dance. All the children joined the 'moonflower' group, then 'grew' into an enormous moonflower. The moonflower shrivelled and collapsed.

Summary

percussion accompaniment
|
grow, shrivel ——— **WANDERING MOON** — four groups
|
twist — turn, circle

run, stop

204

dodge
creep

Although 'dodge' and 'creep' are the initial actions, others - like rolling, leaping, slithering - will be added as the movement is developed. Emphasize the main contrast between moving fast and slowly.

Use imagery which evolves from the movement. A dramatic effect is achieved if half the children are moving fast and the others slowly, simultaneously.

Accompaniment woodblock - dodging
tambour - creeping
or music 'Night Atmosphere' (for jungle) from *BBC Sound Effects*.

Follow up writing or tape recording an adventure story.

Questions and Tasks
1 Sit near me. Watch my hands. Wherever they dodge in the space, you copy (up, down, to the side).
2 Standing. Face me and whichever direction I dodge in, you copy. Ready . . . this way etc.
3 Now listen to the sound of the woodblock. Dodge with the *sound*.
4 Choose which direction you go in. Show me.
5 How fast can you make your feet go? Can you change direction quickly?
6 Listen to the sound of the tambour. Show me slow, slow creeping, close to the ground.
7 Try crawling and creeping, sometimes on your hands and knees, sometimes on your feet.
8 This boy has thought of *slithering*, too. Which part of his body is he moving along on?
9 Everyone practise now crawling, creeping, slithering. Keep on changing the part of your body you are moving on.
10 Keep it slow and careful

11 Listen to the accompaniment now. With the *woodblock* you move fast - dodging, turning, moving up and down in different directions.

With the *tambour* beat you move slowly and carefully, close to the ground.

12 When the sound stops, you stop - high or low - and listen.

13 Now let's have two groups of children: number one group will move on the dodging sound; number two on the creeping sound.

The Dance

The class decides where the movement could be taking place (i.e. a location) - a jungle, a bomb site, a haunted house - and the action sequence is arranged accordingly.

We are on a bomb site. We think we are being pursued. We creep and dodge and listen, then run to safety to the centre of the room.

Summary

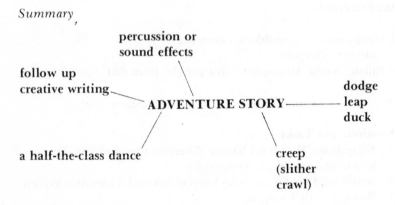

percussion or
sound effects

follow up
creative writing

ADVENTURE STORY

dodge
leap
duck

a half-the-class dance

creep
(slither
crawl)

237 SHAKY KING

This is a story of a king who could not stop shaking. His people thought of many *action* cures. Finally one *did* cure him.

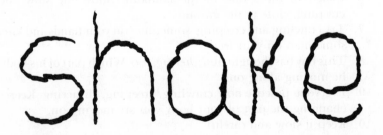

Use *shaking* combined with other actions. Think of 'cures', which use contrasting body parts or qualities. Make a paper-bag puppet of the king. Alternate the puppet shaking with the people moving a 'cure'.

Follow up making king paper-bag puppets.

Questions and Tasks

1 Listen to the shaking sound. Show me how the king can't stop shaking . . .

2 Everyone do:
      shaky runs
      and shaky jumps
      and shaky falling down
      and shake all over
      and STOP.

3 Sit by me. Let's think of a magic movement to cure the king.
      Five claps and a stamp? Ready . . .
      clap, clap, clap, clap, clap, STAMP.
      Galloping on a fast horse? Ready . . .
      . . . and STOP.
      Swimming in cold water? Show me . . .
      . . . and STOP.
      Turning round ten times?
      Swinging his arms? (etc.)

4 Here's the king (the paper-bag puppet). He is shaking and shaking. I am going to play some music now and you are going to dance your 'cures' for the king to see if you can stop him shaking. Here's the music. Which movements shall we begin with?
      A jumping, jumping, jumping cure.

5 And he's still shaking.
      So dance another cure.

The Dance

A teacher (puppet) and class dance
   The puppet shakes and stops.
   The children dance a 'cure'.
   The puppet shakes etc.
until one cure does stop him.

   Alternatively the children can be kings, can shake and stop in a variety of shaky shapes, while a 'people' paper-bag puppet jumps or whirls to cure them.

   While the puppet moves, the children must be still and vice versa.

Summary

a teacher and class
dance

SHAKY KING ──── shaky
runs
jumps
falls etc.

tambourine
accompaniment

action 'cures'

238   STAMPING ELEPHANT

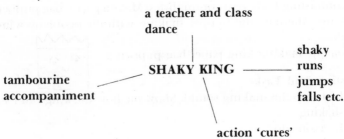

stamp
wriggle
creep

The story in brief

In 'Stamping Elephant' by Anita Hewett in *Tell Me Another Story* (Puffin), Elephant will not stop stamping. Various forest creatures try to cure him. Mouse finally does so by creeping into his trunk while he is asleep and refusing to go until he promises to behave. There are many possible variations of the above idea. Most important is to abstract a *few* movement ideas, so that it is the flow and variety of the *movement* that is paramount, rather than miming the story.

The elephant, the snake or the mouse could each form the basis of a separate lesson. The next lesson might develop the sinuous wriggling movement to a suitable piece of music.

Questions and Tasks

1   Who remembers Elephant? What did he DO?
2   Stay near me. Altogether, three stamps. Stamp, stamp, stamp!
3   Can you finish in a strong shape - strong arms, strong legs?
4   One boy was beating his fists as he stamped. All try that.
5   Ready - creep into your space.

6 Listen to the rhythm on the tambour. Show me some big stamps and stop.

7 Lift your knees and arms high as you stamp. Make yourself large.

8 Now run fast into another space and stop, and into another space and stop.

9 Listen to this fast stamp in rhythm on the tambour. Ready - fast stamping.

10 Good. I saw someone stamping and jumping on two feet, and someone else turning and stamping. How many ways can you find?

11 I've brought a snake (a stocking stuffed with foam rubber) to show you. Sit down and watch me move him. Watch how he wriggles and twists on the floor.

12 You try wriggling and twisting moving as much as you can. Listen to the tambourine. Ready... Watch this child rolling and wriggling, using his knees - all try that.

13 Watch how the snake wriggles high and low. You wriggle high and low.

14 Stand. Altogether, creep whichever way I creep. Stop when I stop.

15 Shake your head up and down, up and down ... and creep slowly to me. Sit slowly.

The Dance

Half the class moves, half the class sounds

After practising and exploring the actions, half the class sits and says:

Stamp, stamp, stamp, along came elephant repeating the phrase many times. The other half moves showing its stamping dance. Then the stamping ones sit and say: Snake wriggled and squirmed, making the words sound like the action, while the other half shows its wriggling dance.

All the children then join in the unison action of no. 15, which simplifies into one movement phrase, the idea of elephant shaking her head, and creeping sadly home.

Summary

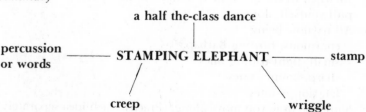

Pictures

239 BARBAPAPA

bouncing
rolling
wriggling

The emphasis here is on growing into a body shape and then *moving* in that shape with humorous results. Select several ideas and practise them altogether so that the children have a variety of movement experiences in the lesson.

Questions and Tasks

1   Listen to the cymbal. Keep on changing your shape. Sometimes you're all round, sometimes you're all long, sometimes . . . You show me.

2   Good. Try once again. You don't have to be on your feet. You can be on your back, your knees . . . This time, every time the sound stops, you stop and let's see *what you look like* . . .

3   Everyone now, *copy* this person's shape. He's balanced on his toes with his arms wide.
    Move now to another space, in that shape. Yes, everyone bounce to another space:
    Bounce, bounce, bounce and stop.

4   Now *change* your shape again. Slowly. What do you look like? Now everyone try *this* shape. He's lying on his side with his leg stretched in the air. Can you *move* in that position? Push and pull yourself along.

5   All try now being:
    enormous, *turning* Barbapapas
    small, tight rolling ones
    sharp, bouncy ones
    fat, floppy ones.
    Show me how you move along. (Practise each idea separately.)

The Dance
A class and teacher dance
Each child begins in a space in a Barbapapa shape. The teacher 'brings the picture alive' by playing on a tambourine amongst the children. They all dance to the sound of her instrument. At a bang on the tambourine they all return to their first shape and finish in stillness.

Summary

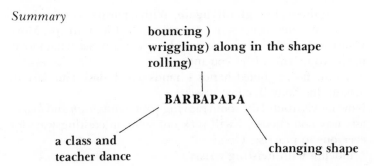

bouncing)
wriggling) along in the shape
rolling)
|
BARBAPAPA

a class and
teacher dance

changing shape

240 HANDS
Photographs might be used as a stimulus. Such as the photograph of 'Hands' in *Junior Voices Book Four* (Penguin Educational)

open
close
dart
press

Explore slow-motion hand movement and quick-pace ones. Use imagery to help develop the movement. Use 'mirroring' partner-work. Choose a vigorous starting activity.

Follow up handprints (using paint) made by different *parts* of the hands; or hand poems.

Questions and Tasks

1 Stand near me. All together in slow motion:
   open your hands
   close them
   twist them.

2 Watch your hands. As they open, stretch them far away from you. Stretch the whole body. As they close, close up the whole body. Curl in.

3 Look at these photographs again. With a partner: one leads the movement, one copies - like seeing yourself in a mirror. Move your hands in the space, like hands in a dream. See what movements your hands lead you into.

4 Try now fast, agitated hands - hands which dash and dart all around the body like fast insects.

5 Now move around the room moving your hands *high* and *low* in any way you choose. I will pick out some interesting ways for everyone to practise. Good:
   moving with twisting wrists
   wriggling fingers
   pressing the palms up and down.

The Dance

A 'hand dance' with a partner. Titles might arise such as: fierce, tired or sad hands.

Summary

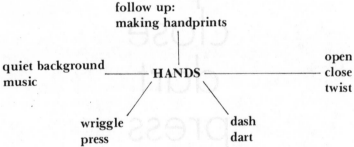

follow up:
making handprints

quiet background
music

HANDS

open
close
twist

wriggle
press

dash
dart

Colourful Locations

241 MARS

walking

'Walking' is a starting point for fantasy. Walking becomes 'getting along'. All kinds of strange travelling can be experimented with, but note that *size, extension* and making *rhythmic sequences* are stressed throughout. Avoid restricted movements - work for flow. Have a brief preparatory discussion near the beginning of the lesson about *how* people or creatures might move on Mars. In this lesson, children's suggestions are starting points. With less-experienced children, the latter might equally well be the teacher's examples.

Accompaniment music, for example *BBC Radiophonic* 'Structures'.

Questions and Tasks

1 'Slowly' is the word I want you to think about. Now, as I point to you, one by one, I want you to walk any way you like *slowly* into a space and stay there very still in any position you think is right for Mars . . .
   Listen to the music. Ready . . .

2 People walked in some very strange ways then. Let's all practise some of them.

3 Try walking high with the fingertips leading you high, really stretched up, then curling down to the ground and up again:
   High, high and *high* and down, down, down, and high . . .
   Good, some people were curling down into a tight, twisted shape, really opening themselves out high and coming right down. Try that again, lots of times.

4 That was a weird one. You were thinking of a green foot? Everyone try his *foot-high-in-the-air* step.

5 Now these big, floppy walks and slide to the ground:
   And walk and walk and slide the hands down, And walk . . .
   as if you have no bones. Yes, make the heads and arms flop as you walk.

6 Lie on the floor very relaxed and still. Now listen to this amount of time. Don't move but when I tap the tambour imagine your movement begins. When I tap again, your movement ends.

7 We have had some really weird walks. Now, with a *partner*, practise a phrase of getting along. Begin and end together in a still position. Ready, I give you a tap on the tambour for your movement beginning. A tap for ending. You move in the silence between the taps. That's how long you have.

The Dance
A partner dance can develop from no. 7 The children can work out a movement sequence and decide where they will dance in relationship to each other. How does their dance end? Think of an action word ending, for example:

disappear
disintegrate
explode!

The following extracts from children's poems show how this dance stimulated writing, phrases from which were used in the next lesson as both movement stimulus and vocal accompaniment:

Floppy and gooey and
Shiny with gold
He goes along upon
His nose.

Tina (8 years)

There he stands twisting
In the moonlight . . .
He is slimy and cold
Now he is off again
Walks on his toes . . .

Summary

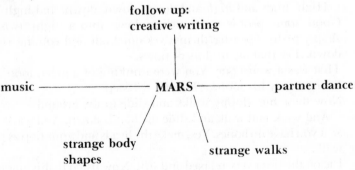

214

float
open, close
dive

Many other actions could be used. It is important to choose a *few* contrasting ideas and deeply explore the sensation of the movement so that it becomes a body rhythm. Note that one idea (nos.2-4) is directed and used to extend the body. The other idea (no.5) gives opportunity for creativity.

Accompaniment 'Water Sounds' from *BBC Sound Effects*.

Questions and Tasks

1   Stand very still in your space. Close your eyes. Imagine floating in warm water. Move gently. The water is so buoyant it holds you up. Floating . . . floating . . . and rest. Some people were moving their elbows, heads, fingers really gently, lightly.

2   Now *swim* in the water. Show me breast-stroke arms. Ready, the hands:

     push upwards, *open* wide and close in downwards
     push up, open and close in.

3   As you push, stretch up as high as you can. As you open, arch the back, be as wide as you can. Make the whole body join in the movement, bend the knees. Keep the movement going. Ready . . .

4   Now step up and down smoothly with breast-stroke arms. Make the movement rise up and sink down. Use your backs.

5   Try it now from a *different position*. See if you can use your legs too. Yes, lie *on your back* and make your legs swim in the air:

     Bend and open and together . . . and then onto your *knees* and close in. Let's all do that idea.

6   Ready for a *diving* position (any diving starting position; stimulate variety) . . .

     and another . . .
     and another . . .

and balance. Can you stay there? There were lots of good ideas then. Hands and one foot on the floor, the other one *stretched* high behind.

A ready-to-dive wide standing position
A dive shape, knee tucked under on the floor.

7 Altogether, try moving into three different dive shapes:
press into a dive shape
press into a dive shape
press into a dive shape.

The Dance
A half-the-class dance
Half the class sits in a large circle (symbolizing the pool). Half the class stands in the circle (ready to jump into the water). As the water sound begins, they jump into the 'pool' (into the circle) and make a swimming dance — opening, closing arms, turning, diving downwards, stretching forwards etc. As the music fades, they return to the edge and hold their position. The groups change over.

A partner dance 'swimming together'.

Summary

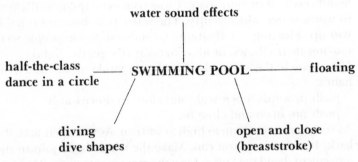

water sound effects

half-the-class
dance in a circle ———— SWIMMING POOL ———— floating

diving   open and close
dive shapes   (breaststroke)

243 TIGHTROPE AND THE HUMAN CANNONBALL

walk balance fall run JUMP

Encourage the children to phrase their own movement, to be aware of moving from one body shape to another. A narrow framework for improvisation is given.

Accompaniment A Sousa march.

Questions and tasks

1 Begin in groups of three. You must watch each other carefully.. Watch these three children:
   The first one stands balanced as if on the end of a tightrope. The other two sit behind him. The first one:
   balances carefully along
   overbalances and
   falls into a really good shape.
As soon as he is still, the second one begins. When the second one has *fallen* off and landed, the third one begins and soon, until all three are sitting. (Demonstrate with the children.)

2 Each of the three now finds a space. Know who is going to be first, second, third. Make it very clear *when* you fall. Ready, the first one walking, balancing . . . (the teacher plays a gentle random background beat, encouraging action with her voice).

3 Good. Each group really tried to make it clear then. Now let's make the movement better. How are you going to step along that tightrope?
   Up and down?
   Stepping and turning?
   Lifting the knees - very proud?
   Everyone practise:
   two steps forward, half-a-turn, and two steps backwards.
   (Practise several ideas with a clear rhythm. Music may help here.)

4 Now try the idea again and make the fall much more exciting. What do the arms do, what do the legs do? Everyone ready to begin. I will give you a starting sound. You show me you have finished by sitting still.

5 Good. We will carry on with that idea next lesson and make it into a dance. Think of those ways of *falling*. To finish up with, let's have two files of children facing each other.

6 The files represent the cannon. The first two stand ready at the top. We (the class and teacher) will give you a rhythm with *clapping:*
   run, run, run, run, run, run, JUMP.
   clap, clap, clap, clap, clap, clap, CLAP.

The first two run down between the files and *jump* as high as you can into the air and then join the end of the files and the next two stand ready. Everyone must help with the rhythm.

The Dance
A group dance for three
Practise and make the movement rhythmic by repeating the sequences and encouraging the children to 'say' their rhythms. Use the words to accompany:

Lift and lift and balance and . . . f a l l.

In a subsequent lesson, balances could be worked on - 'clever balances', involving arms as well as legs.

Summary

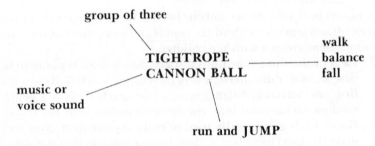

244 THE MACHINE

stretch out, in
press up, down
swing round and
round
jerk forwards

Follow children's suggestions about what machines 'do'. The above can also be used to encourage awareness of space around the body. Children's voice sounds are the best accompaniment. Make the sound start and stop with the movement. But do not introduce voice accompaniment until the movement is clear and controlled. Have a vigorous free-flowing warm up.

Accompaniment voice sound or 'Reggae' from *Your Body Working and Dancing* XX1 209.
Follow up make a junk machine (huge one).

Questions and tasks
1   Sitting near me, not too close to each other, show me with your *hands* the sort of movement your machine does. Yes, everyone try that one:
>   and stretch the hands and grip
>   and out and *in*
>   and out and in.

Make the movement bigger, make it stronger, come to standing and:
>   out and in - and STILL.

That was like a huge grabbing machine.

2   Try another one:
    (press) *up* and *down* and up and down.
    Use your *arms* and *hands*.
    Use your *whole body* (many times).
3   Find a space opposite a partner and face each other. Move together now on the rhythm:
       press *up* and down
       press *up* and down.
    Keep it going. Can you develop it? How can the movement *grow*?
4   Good. Several people added another idea. All try:
  (a) Press *up* with the right hand and *down* with the right hand. Stretch the whole side, go as high and as deep as you can. Then alternate:
       right side, left side.
  (b) Turning as you *press* down
       stretching as you press up.
    There were a lot of other good ideas too. All practise.
5   Let's make a *big flywheel*. Use big *swings* round and round. The movement begins slowly, then gets faster. Use the right arm, then the left arm . . . Now slow it down . . .
6   Who can *jump forwards* like a machine gone wrong?
       Try j e r k y jumps:
       Jump - jump - jump - and JUMP.
    Make your *arms* join in.
7   Everyone lie down. Close your eyes. Remember all the different movements we've had. Think about the best ones.
    Now, with your partner, think how you will begin. Make a short machine dance. Give it a title.

The Dance

A partner dance as above - the ideas may be selected from several lessons.

Practising Voice Sounds

'All sit near me. As I make the up-down piston movement with my arm, you make the sound. When I stop, you stop.' (Have half the class moving a piston arm, half the class sounding.)

In the same way, humming 'circular' sounds, or making *jerky* sounds could be tried.

When the children add sound to their own movement, they can do so quietly, so that the sound accents rather than dominates. It does not need to be loud.

Summary

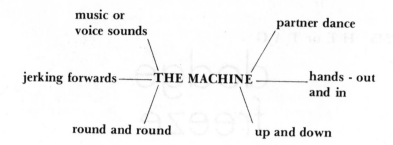

music or
voice sounds

partner dance

jerking forwards —— THE MACHINE ——hands - out
and in

round and round

up and down

Games

245   H E or T A G

dodge
freeze

Use 'He' or 'Tag' as a movement framework. Emphasize body parts *dodging* and body shape *stopping*. Organize four groups before the lesson. Do a slow, stretching warm up.

Questions and Tasks

1   Sit near me. The first group find a space in *this half* of the hall. The second group find a space in the other half of the hall.

2   Both groups have a 'He' person . . . that's you and you. Both groups must stay in their half of the room. When I play the tambour, each group plays 'He'. When the tambour stops, everyone freezes. Ready . . . Move really fast.

3   Come and sit by me. The third and fourth group spread out. You do the same thing but I want everyone to move much more. Everyone:
      dodge one way, the other way
      duck down
      step to the side.
   Make it look as if you are all being chased all the time. When you are touched, you *freeze*. Ready . . .

4   Hold those positions really still. Can you see the different ways they've *stopped* - some high, some low, someone just about to turn, caught in mid-action.

5   (Improving) Everyone find a space. Whichever body *part of you* I call out, move it out of the way in the space, stretch it away as if that is the part that I am going to touch. Ready:
      Head! Elbow! Knee!
   Good, some people got themselves into really dramatic positions.

6   Let's make it a slow motion 'He', as if you were being chased in a dream. slow motion, Ready . . . move between each other carefully.

7   All try that one. Lean right forward. Good, someone there did a
     slow-motion swerve to the side.

The Dance
Dream 'He'

Two groups move at a time so that the children have plenty of space:
  (a) fast-moving 'He', dodging and stopping
  (b) slow-motion 'He', big, slow movements
  (c) when touched, slowly collapse to the ground.
Let each group evolve its own idea. Provide the above framework if
necessary.

Summary

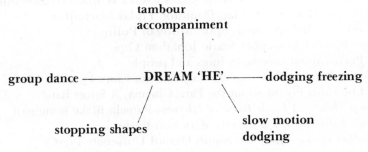

Appendices

A LIST OF POETRY BOOKS FOR DANCE

That Way and This Poetry for Creative Dance Frances
  Baldwin and Margaret Whitehead Chatto Windus
A Puffin Quartet of Poets Kaye Webb (ed)
Rhyme and Rhythm Blue Book Gibson and Wilson Macmillan
Roundabout Six Margaret Rawlins Frederick Warne
There's Motion Everywhere John Travers Moore Nelson
Junior Voices 1-4 Geoffrey Summerfield Penguin Education
Wordscapes Barry Maybury Oxford University Press
Complete Poems for Children James Reeves William Heinemann
Poems to Hear and See Ian Hamilton Finlay Macmillan
A Book of Milliganimals Spike Milligan Puffin
Fire Words Christopher Searle Jonathan Cape
  Poems about moods, feelings and people
Tower Blocks - Poems of the City Marion Lines Franklin Watts
  Colourful Poems about the Fair, Cinema, A Street Band.
Peep Show - A Little Book of Rhymes Pamela Blake Longman
This Little Puffin Elizabeth Matterson Puffin
Mother Goose Brian Wildsmith Oxford University Press

BIBLIOGRAPHY

Charlie and the Chocolate Factory Roald Dahl Puffin
Children Make Sculpture Elizabeth Leyh Van Rostrand Reinhold
Festivals Ruth Manning Sanders Heinemann
Groves Dictionary of Music and Musicians
How to Make Masks Michael Kingsley Skinner Studio Vista
Larousse Encyclopedia of Mythology
Maori Myths and Tribal Legends A. Alpers John Murray
Mother Goose Brian Wildsmith Oxford University Press
Mr Men Books Roger Hargreaves Thurman Ltd.
My Friend Mr Leakey J.B.S. Haldane
Norwegian Fairy Tales F. Muller
Shells in Colour Dr. R.T. Abbott Penguin
Tell Me another Story Eileen Colwell Puffin
The Flying Machine O. Postgate and P. Firmin Kaye Ward Ltd.
The Foot Book Dr Seuss Collins Harvill
The Great Blueness Arnold Lobel
The Lore and Language of Schoolchildren Iona and Peter Opie
  Oxford University Press

The Musical Instrument Recipe Book Penguin Educational
The Snowy Day Ezra Jack Keats Picture Puffin
Volcanoes HMSO Publication
World History of the Dance Curt Sachs W. W. Norton

USEFUL FURTHER READING

The Art and Science of Creativity George F. Kneller Holt, Rinehart
and Winston
The Foundations of Language Andrew Wilkinson Oxford
University Press
Knowing in My Bones Ruth Foster A. & C. Black
Movement Awareness and Creativity Lea Bartal and Nira Neeman
Souvenir Press
Teaching Creative Movement Johanna Exiner and Phyllis Lloyd
Angus and Robertson

MUSIC LIST

Bach	Brandenburg Concerto No. 2 in F
Bartok	Roumanian Dances
Bartok	'For Children' Piano solos
Bartok	'Out of Doors' Piano pieces
Berlioz	Roman Carnival
Berlioz	Jeux d'Enfants
Bizet	L'Arlesienne Suite
Blades James	'Blades on Percussion' DIS ABK 135
	(lively extracts - various composers)

BBC records and cassettes

	'Atmospheric Sound Effects' REC 225
	'Bang on a Drum' cassette MRMC 004
	'Music from Children's Programmes' REH 214
	'BBC Radiophonic' REC 25
	'Sound Effects' Records No.3 RED 102 M
	'John Peel's Archive Things' REC 68 M
Britten B.	Sea Interludes from *Peter Grimes*
Britten B.	Young Person's Guide to the Orchestra
Cage John	'Strange Amores' from Voices Record 2
	2 Argo DA 94
Copland A.	Rodeo
Davies Maxwell	'Turris Campamarum Sonantium'
	percussion and pre-recorded tapes 01S DSLO 1
Debussy	'Le Vent d'Ouest' from Piano Preludes Book I
Debussy	'Printemps'

Downes Bob	'Open Music'	BDOM 001
Elgar	'Troyte' from 'Enigma Variations'	
Eight American Dances		EP 538
Fairground Music		AMB AFL
Falla	'Ritual Fire Dance' from 'El Amor Brujo'	
Faure	'Pavane' Flute Solo	
Granados	Spanish dance, Andaluza	
Ghanaian Music	'Mustapha Tetty Addy' drumming	
		TAN TGS113
Greek Folk Music	'The Magic of Greece'	RED Z5 134
Ibert	'Clowns Dance for Orchestra'	HMV CLP 1409
Kodaly	Dances of Galanta	ACL 75
Liadov	Baba Yaga	
Listen Move and Dance Records nos. 1-3		CLP 3762
	No. 4	CLP 3531
Maori Songs	'Traditional Maori Songs'	ORYX EXP 53
'Mediaeval Music'	Cl. 1300	TEL SAWT 9504
Mendelssohn	Scherzo from music for 'Midsummer Night's Dream'	
Mexican Music	'The Folklore of Mexico'	POL 545 013
'Modern Primitive Beginners' (drumming) Gamba Educational		
		DCG 011
Mozart	'Twelve German Dances for Orchestra'	
		DEC LXT 6132
Mussorgsky	Night on the Bare Mountain	
Oldfield Mike	Tubular Bells	
'Playtime' songs and rhymes		SH M818
Prokofiev	March from 'Love of Three Oranges' and numerous piano pieces	
Poulenc	Flute Sonata on 'Listen Move and Dance' 1-3	
Ravel	Mother Goose Suite	
Rimsky Korsakov	'Capriccio Espagnol	
'Ring of Iron'	Folk Songs	TSR 016
Rossini-Respighi	La Boutique Fantasque	
Saint-Saens	Carnival of the Animals	
Seaside Song	'Oh, I do like to be beside the seaside'	
Sea Songs and Shanties'		TOP TPS 205
Seeger Pete	'Abiyoyo and Other Story Songs for Children'	
	cassette	XCXTR 1066 XTRA
Sousa	'Famous Sousa Marches'	RCA INTS 1332
Stravinsky	Le Baiser de la Fee	
'The World of Folk'		SPA A 132

'Voices'	Four Records, First Book (poems, songs, music)	Argo DA 91
Walton	Facade	
Warlock	Capriol Suite	
'Your Body Working and Dancing'		XX1 209 PE 7 & 8

SUMMARY OF FOLLOW-UP ACTIVITIES

Parts I and II

16   Drawing and labelling 'Action bodies'
62   Language/movement games.
63   Making patterns with words, paint and string
66 - 69
83   Making costumes
111   Collecting things on a class walk
115   Making sculptures
122   Collecting advertisements
148   Making 'Chinese' costumes and masks

Lessons

187   Reading poem 'Little Leaf Falls'
189   Humming sounds - tape recorded
192   Collecting things which bounce, spin, roll etc.
        e.g. marbles, sycamore seeds
198   Talking and 'Frog' words
204   Clown noses out of egg box sections
        Clown newspaper collages
205   Red Indian headdresses
206   Witch costumes and masks
207   Anger masks out of cardboard plates
208   Cat poems recording a cat purr
209   Collage crocodile
210   Dinosaur box sculpture and drawings
213   Rain poems
214   Hot colours - tissue paper collage, sun poem
223   Bounce, spin finger painting
224   Drum rhythms - tape recorded
225   Drawing different kinds of feet
227   Collecting pictures of animals or moving things
230   Making small 'shakers'

Index

(The numbers in this index refer to paragraph numbers and *not* to page numbers.)

Notes on the Cassette to Accompany this Book

Music composed by Roger North

Music may be used at any point in the lesson, for example to accompany starting activities, creative work or a completed dance. One piece only might be used, or two contrasting pieces chosen for the lesson (see paragraphs **30, 47** and **48**).

The order of the music on the tape is arbitrary but there is contrast from piece to piece. The last two pieces are more suited to older children. The length of each piece is intended for ease of practice without the need to rewind the tape. A part of one piece only might well accompany a whole dance.

Each piece is preceded by a spoken title. The title indicates a suitable basic action or image and the action words below give examples of other movements that may develop. The music may be linked with many sections in the book. *Some* of these are included under 'Paragraph References'. The emphasis is on action words. The teacher or children may well relate these to any appropriate image or situation (see paragraphs **38-45**).

MUSIC TITLES SIDE ONE	MOVEMENT SUGGESTIONS
1 BODY RHYTHM	Body part movement. Head rolling, shoulder shrugging, feet jumping, tapping and stepping. Arms swinging or thrusting. Middle section - wind sound & rhythm: fluid arm movements, whirling or rolling. **(see paragraphs 16, 120, 162, 165, 167, 244).**
2 LIGHTNESS	Rising up, drifting down, floating, balancing, turning, soft jumps, delicate hand movements. **(see paragraphs 17, 74, 84, 103, 193a and b).**
3 PIED PIPER	Gay, fast pace sequences of jumps, skips, hops and turns. Staccato feet, hand or back movements. Speeded up movements for humorous effects. **(see paragraphs 13, 84, 86, 88, 204).**
4 DODGING and STOPPING	(a) Fast *travelling* and sudden stops, using different directions and different starting and stopping positions.

236

(b) **Dodging:** the feet, hands or head while staying *on the spot*.

(c) A dodging *dance* including other sudden movements: rolls, leaps, turns.

(see paragraphs 15, 58, 63, 140, 156, 245).

5 CREEPING and PAUSING
Large movements, creeping, stretching crawls, rolls or slithers. Pausing and balancing in different positions. Try moving fast in *contrast* with the accompaniment.

(see paragraphs 58, 97, 188).

6 BUBBLES
Make bubble body shapes (round shapes). Move along in them. Make group shapes, burst them. Copy the quality of the music with undulating, jerking, strange ways of travelling.

(see paragraphs 72, 97, 141).

SIDE TWO

7 BOUNCING
Bouncing, skipping, galloping, hopping and flopping. Jumps with foot taps, flicks and kicks.

(see paragraphs 28, 63, 75, 86, 173, 223).

8 STRETCHING
Opening out, gripping in, elongating, twisting, balancing. Long stretching steps and turns, slow stretched out falls, contrasted with occasional sudden movement.

(see paragraphs 18, 64, 69, 72, 141, 197).

9 ROCKING
Swaying, swinging arms leading to turning and leaping. Swing the hips into tumble and roll. Make up swaying step patterns.

(see paragraphs 75, 134, 187, 198).

10 LEAPING, LEAPING
Up in the air movement. Toss, turn and leap. Crouch, stretch upwards. Run and explode.

(see paragraphs 58, 100, 182, 219).

11 WIND
Move as if being blown by wind. Toss up and collapse down. Turn and press down. Spin quickly and stop. Leap and leap and leap. Press outwards, then whirl suddenly to another spot. Sway gently.

(see paragraphs 102, 107, 108, 217).

12 DRAMATIC DANCE
Partner work. Watch and respond to each other's movement. Opening wide, closing up, large strong arm movements, rising up strongly etc.

(see paragraphs 40, 60, 80, 84, 207).

13 NIGHTMARE   Rushing, running, darting, falling, retreating, struggling. Or mechanical movements which enlarge.
(see paragraphs 140, 156, 162).